Young People's Science Encyclopedia

Ra

Radiation
Radiation, biological effects
Radiation detector
Radiation, protection
Radiation, uses of
Radical, chemical
Radicle
Radio
Radio telescope
Radio tube
Radioactive elements
Radioactivity
Radiograph
Radiosonde
Radish
Radium
Radon
Raffia
Ragweed
Rain gauge
Rain making
Rainbow
Ramie
Range finder
Raoult's Law
Rapid
Raptures of the deep
Rare-earth elements
Rarefaction
Rarefied air
Raspberry
Rat
Ratio
Rattan
Raven
Ray
Ray, alpha
Ray, beta
Ray, cosmic
Ray, gamma
Ray, infrared
Ray, ultraviolet
Rayon

Re

Reagent
Real image
Receptors
Recessive
Rectum
Recycling
Redbud
Reducing agent
Reduction
Redwood
Reed
Reed, Walter
Reef
Reflection
Refraction
Refractory
Refrigeration
Regeneration
Reinforced concrete
Relapse
Relativity
Reproduction, asexual
Reproduction, sexual
Reproductive systems
Reptilia
Research
Reservoir
Resin
Resistance
Resolution
Resonance
Respiratory system
Resuscitation
Retrograde motion
Revolution

Rh

Rh factor
Rhenium
Rheostat
Rheumatic fever
Rhinoceros
Rhizome

Rhodium
Rhododendron
Rhubarb

Ri

Rice
Richards, Dickenson
Richardson, Sir Owen
Richter Scale
Ridge
Rift valley
Ringworm
River

Ro

Robbins, Frederick
Robin
Robinson, Sir Robert
Robot
Rocket
Rocket engine
Rocket propellant
Rocket sled
Rocks
Rodent
Roe
Roentgen, Wilhelm
Root
Rootworm
Rope
Rose
Rosemary
Rose-of-Sharon
Rosewood
Ross, Sir Ronald
Rot
Rotation
Rotifera
Rotor

Ru

Rubber
Rubber, synthetic

Rubber plant
Rubidium
Rubidium-strontium dating
Ruby
Ruminant
Runner
Rust
Rusting
Rutabaga
Ruthenium
Rutherford, Ernest

Rye

Sa

Saccharin
Saffron
Sage
Sagebrush
Sagittarius
Saint Vitus dance
Salamander
Salivary glands
Salk, Jonas
Salmon
Salt
Saltpeter
Salve
Salvia
Samarium
Sand
Sand dollar
Sandalwood
Sandarac
Sandbar
Sandblast
Sandpiper
Sandworm
Sanitation
Sansevieria
Saponification
Sapphire
Saprophyte
Sapsucker
Sapwood
Sardine
Sargassum
Sassafras

YOUNG PEOPLE'S
SCIENCE ENCYCLOPEDIA

Edited by the Staff of
NATIONAL COLLEGE OF EDUCATION, Evanston, Illinois

ASSOCIATE EDITORS

HELEN J. CHALLAND, B.E., M.A., Ph.D.
  Chairman, Division of Natural Sciences
  National College of Education,
  Evanston, Illinois

DONALD A. BOYER, B.S., M.S., Ph.D.
  Science Education Consultant, Winnetka
  Public Schools, Winnetka, Illinois
  Science, National College of Education

EDITORIAL CONSULTANTS
ON THE STAFF OF NATIONAL COLLEGE OF EDUCATION

Elizabeth R. Brandt, B.A., M.Ed.
Eugene B. Cantelupe, B.A., M.F.A., Ph.D.
John H. Daugherty, B.S., M.A.
Irwin K. Feinstein, B.S., M.A., Ph.D.
Mary Gallagher, A.B., M.A., Ph.D.
Beatrice S. Garber, A.B., M.S., Ph.D.
Hal S. Galbreath, B.S. Ed., M.S.
Arthur J. Hannah, B.S., M.Ed., Ed.D.

Robert R. Kidder, A.B., M.A., Ph.D.
Jean C. Kraft, B.S., M.A., Ph.D.
Elise P. Lerman, B.A., B.F.A., M.F.A.
Mary M. Lindquist, B.A., M.A., Ph.D.
Mary-Louise Neumann, A.B., B.S.L.S.
Lavon Rasco, B.A., M.A., Ph.D.
Bruce Allen Thale, B.S.Ed., M.S.Ed.
Fred R.Wilkins, Jr., B.A., M.Ed., Ph.D.

SPECIAL SUBJECT AREA CONSULTANTS

Krafft A. Ehricke, B.A.E., H.L.D.
Benjamin M. Hair, A.B., M.D.
Charles B. Johnson, B.S., M.A., M.S.
Raymond J. Johnson, B.B.A., M.Ed.

H. Kenneth Scatliff, M.D.
Eleanor S. Segal, M.D.
Paul P. Sipiera, B.A., M.S.
Ray C. Soliday, B.A., B.S., M.A. (Deceased)

Don Dwiggins, Aviation Editor

THE STAFF

Project Director	Rudolph A. Hastedt
Project Editor	M. Frances Dyra
Senior Editor	Jim Hargrove
Editorial Assistant	Janet Zelasko

Young People's
SCIENCE
Encyclopedia

Edited by the Staff of
NATIONAL COLLEGE OF EDUCATION
Evanston, Illinois

Volume 15/Ra-Sa

CHILDRENS PRESS ™

CHICAGO

Photographs

Page 2:   Skylab space station (NASA)

Page 3:   *Top to Bottom:*
Wheatfield (U.S.D.A. Photo)
Technician capping Abbokinase (Abbott Laboratories)
Spider (Macmillan Science Company)
View of Earth (NASA)
Space Shuttle (NASA)
Bahama coral reef (Macmillan Science Company)

Cover: Design by Sandra Gelak
Biological Spectrograph (Argonne National Laboratory)
Rooster: Old Fat William (James P. Rowan)
Jefferson Salamander (James P. Rowan)
Library of Congress Catalog Card Number: 67-17925

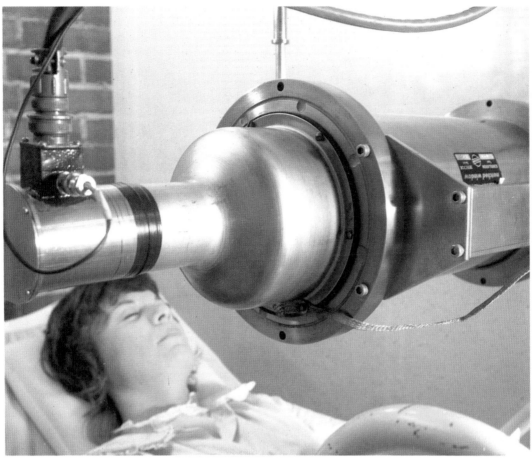

Sensitive crystals in this radiation detector measure small amounts of radiation in the human body.

Radiation. Radiation is energy that can be transferred from one body of material to another across empty space. Radiant energy seems to have a double nature. It behaves as *continuous waves* when it moves swiftly through space. Yet this same energy also acts like particles—such as when it bursts into or out of matter.

In the action of bursting into or out of matter, energy is given off or absorbed in definite packets or unit amounts. Each unit amount is a *quantum* of energy. The energy particles are called *photons*. When moving outside an atom, a photon acts like a wave. It can bend when passing through a lens; it can be reflected; and it can be *diffracted*—made to create a new set of waves when the original wave particle passes through a narrow slit.

ELECTROMAGNETIC ENERGY

Since the late nineteenth century, our knowledge about the properties of radiation and its interactions with matter has been growing steadily. To begin, radiant energy comes in many forms and is often characterized by the region to which it belongs in the ELECTROMAGNETIC SPECTRUM. Beginning at the spectrum's highest energy boundary, one finds *cosmic rays, gamma rays,* and x RAYS. Working down the spectrum in a direction of increasing wavelength, one encounters *ultraviolet radiation, visible light, infrared radiation, microwaves,* and *radio waves.* Regardless of type, all these radiant-energy forms travel as photonwaves through space at the same speed—186,000 miles (about 300,000 kilometers) per second.

At the beginning of this century, the renowned physicists Max Planck and ALBERT EINSTEIN observed that electromagnetic

Radiation

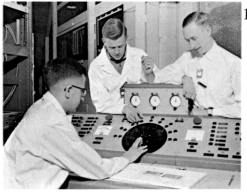

Argonne National Laboratory Photograph

Control board of atomic reactor, a man-made radiation device

radiation is not emitted as a continuous flow of energy. Instead it appears as a shower of independent waves. And each wave contains a small packet of energy. A single discrete energy wave is known as a PHOTON. The package of energy associated with it is a *quantum* of energy.

Planck discovered that the quantum of energy associated with any one photon—its *photon energy*—is proportional to the frequency of the electromagnetic radiation, as described by the equation $E = hv$, where E = the photon energy measured in *ergs*, h = a constant (known as Planck's constant—6.62×10^{-27} ergs per second), and v = the frequency of the radiation (measured in the number of waves per second). Simply, this formula expresses the discovery that the shorter the wavelength is for any type of energy, the more energy its photon carries.

There are no sharp borders between types of radiant energy—cosmic rays merge into gamma rays, which merge into X rays, and so on. What is more, a single radiation source may emit many forms of radiation simultaneously. For example, mercury-vapor incandescent light bulbs emit both ultraviolet light and visible light.

IONIZING RADIATION

The radiant energy forms one most naturally thinks of when the term *radiation* is used are *ionizing radiations*. Electromagnetic radiations whose wavelengths are shorter than ultraviolet light—cosmic rays, gamma rays, and X rays—have two unique characteristics. First, they penetrate easily those materials that are normally *opaque* (totally shielded) to other radiations. More important, particularly to living systems, the photon energies of these radiations are high enough to dislodge virtually any of an

atom's orbiting electrons. Because electrons have a negative electric charge, their absence leaves irradiated atoms with a net positive electric charge. These charged partial atoms (electron-deficient atoms) are known as *ions*.

All ionizing radiations are not electromagnetic energy, however. Certain nuclear, or *elementary particles*, when set in motion by photons or other particles, can produce energy effects called *particle radiations*. Particle radiations are ionizing radiations. For a stream of particles to be ionizing, however, they must be highly energized.

Thus, when electrons move slowly, usually through a conductor such as a copper wire, they produce a low-voltage electric current; when these low-mass particles are given considerably more energy, and as a result more speed, they move through space in a manner similar to photon radiation. The electrons are then known as *cathode* or *beta rays*, or alternatively as *beta radiation*. In similar fashion, helium nuclei at high speeds become *alpha radiation* or *alpha particles*. Still another form of particle radiation is *neutron radiation*, formed by a highly energetic source of neutron particles. Like alpha and beta particles, neutrons may be ejected from atoms undergoing *fission* or *radioactive decay*. Certain high-energy particle accelerators can also produce fast streams of neutrons. Of all ionizing particles, neutrons are the most energetic. This also means that for living systems they present the greatest biological hazard.

NATURAL RADIOACTIVITY

Radioactivity is a property of unstable atoms that causes them to spontaneously alter the precise arrangement, composition, or energy content of their nuclei. The event that causes a nuclear transformation of this type is called *radioactive disintegration* or *radioactive decay*. When an unstable atom undergoes this "decay," it sheds electromagnetic radiation and/or particle radiation.

In 1896, HENRI BECQUEREL and MARIE AND PIERRE CURIE discovered minerals containing a new element, which they named URANIUM. It was then that the first naturally radioactive substance became known. Since that time, about a dozen other elements that spontaneously emit nuclear radiation have been found.

Since uranium's discovery, about a dozen other naturally occurring elements that

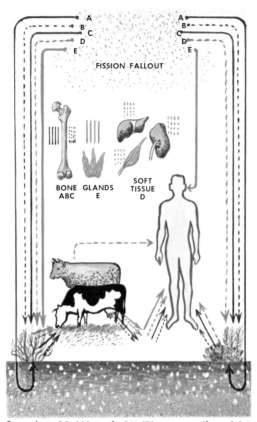

FISSION FALLOUT

BONE
ABC

GLANDS
E

SOFT
TISSUE
D

Strontium-89 (A) and -90 (B) enter soil and become concentrated by plant metabolism. Man
eats plants and plant products and the strontium enters human systems. Cesium-137 (C)
contaminates surface leaves and enters the system the same way. Barium-40 (D) and iodine-131
(E) contaminate the surface and air. All these
isotopes become centered in certain parts of
man's system

Monitoring the top of a nuclear reactor with a
Geiger counter.

spontaneously emit nuclear radiation have
been found. Some of these decay fast;
others very slowly. The radioactive ISOTOPE
(radioisotope) potassium-40, for example,
emits beta and gamma radiation as it decays
with a HALF-LIFE of 1.3 billion years. (A half-
life is the time it takes for half of any quantity of a radioisotope to decay into another
form.) Radioactive carbon — carbon-14 —
has a half-life of 5,730 years. To indicate the
contrast in half-lives possible for similar
elements, consider potassium-42, which
decays with a half-life of only 12.42 hours.
Man has found no way to control the decay
rates of radioisotopes. The energy of these
isotopes can be directed however, and used
for such purposes as dating ancient fossils
or historical artifacts.

SOURCES OF RADIATION

Radiation comes from a variety of sources,
which can be grouped into two general categories: radiation from natural sources and
radiation from human activity.

All living systems are subject to *background radiation,* which comes from natural
sources. Incoming cosmic rays from space
are one unavoidable source of this radiation.
Flying on an airplane or living in geographi-
cal regions of high altitude—where there is
less of earth's atmosphere to screen out these
rays—results in higher doses of exposure.
Other sources of background radiation are
radioisotopes emitted from rocks and soil.
One of the major producers of this radiation
is RADON, a colorless, odorless gas. Radon is
part of the decay chain of uranium, and it
seeps into houses and buildings through
cracks in the foundations. Inhaled radon
decays to alpha particles in the lungs and
causes damage and cancer.

Scientists have also learned how to harness and produce radiation for commercial
use. For humans, the major source of exposure to this nonnatural radiation is medical
and dental X rays. The rest comes from
sources such as radios, watches with luminous dials, and color television sets and
computer monitors.   D.A.B./M.K.H.

SEE ALSO: NUCLEAR SCIENCE; QUANTUM
MECHANICS; RADIATION, BIOLOGICAL EFFECTS
OF; RADIATION, PROTECTION FROM; RADIATION
DETECTOR; SPACE

Testing tracer isotope carbon-14 on kidney bean plants (after 33 days): left, leaves grown in air; middle, leaves grown in light dose of carbon-14 gas; right, leaves grown in heavy dose

Radiation, biological effects All life on earth depends on radiation from the sun. Green plants provide the most visible example of ways in which living systems depend upon radiated energy. Through a process called PHOTOSYNTHESIS, plants harness solar radiation—sunlight—to make food, build new tissue, and power the transport mechanisms that move material through a plant.

Living organisms are selective in the forms of radiation they can use best and in the doses that promote their growth and well-being. For example, humans may benefit from exposure to sunlight in small doses. But when an overdose occurs, a harmful sunburn results.

The most harmful form of radiation to humans is *ionizing radiation.* When ionizing radiation passes through body tissue, it may disrupt the chemical process of the CELLS that make up the tissue, causing the cells to grow abnormally or to die. This cell damage can make an individual ill *(somatic effects)* or harm future descendants *(genetic effects).*

Both the amount and type of radiation to which a person is exposed can determine its relative degree of hazard. The biological damage produced in the human body by different types of ionizing radiation is measured in units called *rems.* A person can receive a dose of up to 25 rems of radiation without showing any immediate effects. Higher doses can cause *radiation sickness,* and doses of more than 800 rems are fatal.

The rate at which a radiation exposure is received can make it more or less dangerous. Scientists have shown that the ability of *fission* (fast) neutrons to transform cells, and potentially damage them, depends on the rate at which a given low-level dose of radiation is administered. Strangely, the slower the dose is delivered, the more dangerous are its effects.

SOMATIC EFFECTS

When ionizing radiation passes through a cell, the *high-energy particles* that are emitted can displace electrons in the cell's atoms. The process can damage the cell's DNA, which holds the information needed for the cell to reproduce. The cell may lose its ability to reproduce, or it may reproduce incorrectly.

Cells that reproduce frequently—such as those in bone marrow—are hurt most by radiation. High radiation doses can cause LEUKEMIA, a disease where the white blood cells multiply abnormally, and CANCER.

In general, exposure to radiation causes a shortening of life. Radiation also appears to lower immunity to disease, damages connective tissue, and causes premature aging. Radiation sickness produces nausea, vomiting, diarrhea, infection, hair loss, and cancer. It can be deadly. *Radiation injuries,* which are localized effects such as burns and hair loss, occur from overdoses of less powerful kinds of radiation. *Radiation poisoning* occurs when radioactive materials are swallowed, inhaled, or injected. Radiation from material inside a body is many times more harmful than external radiation.

GENETIC EFFECTS

Living cells contain large numbers of tiny hereditary units called genes. Pairs of genes determine the characteristics transmitted from parent to child. Ionizing radiation can change genes so that new characteristics not possessed by the parent are handed down to children. Such changes in genes are called MUTATIONS. Only mutations in the reproductive cells of the parent are passed to later generations. Most such mutations in humans are harmful. Inescapable *background radiation* causes some mutations. Any additional exposure to other forms of radiation will cause further damage. This damage is cumulative. The greater the total amount of radiation received by a parent, the greater the possibility of changing the characteristics inherited by the child. Apparently there is no small amount of ionizing radiation that is completely harmless. R.C.S./M.K.H.

SEE ALSO: RADIATION; RADIATION, USES; RADIATION, PROTECTION

Radiation detectors Radiation can be detected and measured using a variety of devices. Some devices record the paths of nuclear particles as they move through space. Other devices detect *ionizing radiation* and emit a signal whenever a particle or photon enters the device. Three common devices used to detect ionizing radiation are (1) Geiger counters, (2) scintillation counters, and (3) solid-state detectors.

GEIGER COUNTERS

The GEIGER COUNTER is one of the most common devices used to detect radiation. It consists of a metal tube filled with a gas at low pressure. A long, thin wire runs through the center of the tube. A high voltage is applied between the wire and the tube. When a particle or photon enters the tube, it produces a brief pulse of electric current. This pulse triggers an electronic counter, which clicks each time a particle is detected. Thus, the number of clicks indicates the intensity of the radiation.

SCINTILLATION COUNTERS

A scintillation counter consists of a crystal attached to a special tube called a *photomultiplier.* The crystal emits a flash of light when radiation passes through it. The photomultiplier detects the flash of light and emits an electric signal in response. Each signal is sent to a counter. The number of signals produced is proportional to the energy of the radiation.

SOLID-STATE DETECTORS

Solid-state detectors are made from *semiconductor diodes.* These diodes consist of electronic circuits etched into pieces of silicon or germanium. When a particle passes through the detector, it generates a pulse of electric current, which can be measured with an electric counter. Solid-state detectors are less effective than other types because most of the particles do not pass through the sensitive region of the device. M.K.H.

SEE ALSO: ELECTRONICS; GEIGER COUNTER

Checking for radioactivity at the surface of a shielded storage vault using a Geiger counter; the technician wears a radiation-detector film badge clipped to his pocket

Daniel Oldfield; Argonne Hosp., U. of Chicago, USAEC

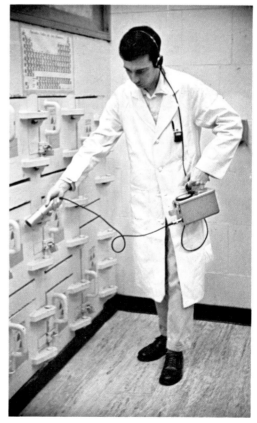

Daniel Oldfield; Argonne Hosp., U. of Chicago, USAEC

A special shielding window is used to prevent the penetration of radiation from particle accelerators used in medical treatment through the glass. The glass is filled with a saturated solution of zinc bromide

Daniel Oldfield; Argonne Hosp., U. of Chicago, USAEC

Radioactive material can be handled with tongs behind a wall of lead bricks. The operator can see behind the wall by looking at the tilted mirror mounted above and to the rear of the bricks

Radiation, protection When people are exposed to radiation, the energy emitted can cause severe biological damage. The amount of damage depends on several factors, including the type and energy of the radiation and the length of exposure. Humans cannot escape radiation entirely, because it is everywhere, but they should guard against unnecessary exposures.

There are several ways to protect a person from exposure to radiation. One simple way is to limit the period of exposure to the radiation. Another method is to increase the distance between the person and the source of the radiation. As the distance increases, the intensity of the radiation decreases. For example, tripling the distance from a radioactive source decreases the radiation the person receives to one-ninth the dose that otherwise would have been received. A third safeguard involves the use of shielding materials, which limit the amount of radiation reaching a person by absorbing the radiation energy. Lead is the most effective shielding material. It absorbs most types of radiation, protecting people from excessive exposure.

In daily life, people are exposed to radiation from two sources: background radiation, such as sunlight and RADON, and radiation from human-made objects. In most places on earth, more than three-fourths of all the radiation people are exposed to is produced naturally. Although some exposure to background radiation is unavoidable, people should take precautions to protect themselves from exposure as much as possible. For example, excessive solar radiation can be avoided by limiting exposure to direct sunlight or by wearing *sunscreens,* lotions which help shield the skin and body. The strongest sunscreens provide the most protection.

The radioactive element RADIUM decays to become radon, a poisonous gas. Radon produced below the surface of the earth can enter homes and other buildings through cracks in the soil and in ground water. Ventilated buildings with well-sealed ground floors lessen exposure to radon, if it is present in the ground.

Radiation produced by humans tends to be a more dangerous form of radiation, known as *ionizing radiation.* Ionizing radiation can cause cell damage, radiation sickness, and death. *Alpha rays, beta rays, gamma rays, X rays,* and *neutrons* are all forms of ionizing radiation. Everyday sources of this type of radiation include smoke detectors and television sets, as well as medical and dental X rays. Nuclear power plants and weapons also generate radiation.

Thin lead aprons are used to shield patients from excessive exposure to medical and dental X rays. It is important that children, pregnant patients, and men and women of child-bearing age are protected each time they have an X ray examination. In addition, unnecessary X rays should be avoided.

Consumer products can emit low levels of radiation. Equipment that emits radiation should be properly labeled with a warning. Someone using such equipment should try

The manipulator is called *master-slave* because every movement that the operator makes is duplicated by the mechanical controls inside the shielded "hot cave"

Daniel Oldfield; Argonne Hosp., U. of Chicago, USAEC

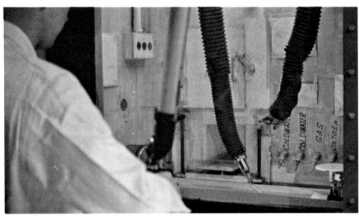

One type of equipment that enables scientists to work with radioactive material without being exposed to radiation is the "master-slave" manipulator.

to stay a reasonable distance away from the object. For example, when watching television or a color computer monitor, the viewer should sit several feet back from the screen.

Many people, particularly scientists and medical technicians, now work in laboratories and power plants where nuclear reactions produce radiation on a large scale. In such places radiation becomes a serious hazard. However, workers in national laboratories and nuclear power plants may be safer than most people, because they are usually shielded adequately from the radiation. Heavy materials are placed around nuclear reactors and X ray machines to absorb the energy of the radiation before it reaches workers. Concrete, lead, iron, earth, wood, and water are convenient, inexpensive materials suitable for shielding. In designing a nuclear reactor, the thickness of any shielding material required for protection can be calculated. In modern X ray equipment, operators stand behind suitable shielding or leave the room while the equipment is being used.

People who work with radiation also take extra precautions. Everyone who works near radiation wears a *dosimeter,* a device that measures the doses of radiation received over a period of time. Personnel check their dosimeters regularly to detect exposure approaching dangerous levels. In some jobs, workers use mechanical hands or remote-control devices to handle radioactive substances.

Much research has been directed toward learning more about the effects of radiation upon living things. The mechanisms by which radiation damages living tissue are under continuous study, with interest centered upon those cells that transmit inherited characteristics. It seems possible that harmless chemical elements or isotopes can be substituted biologically for those that are radioactive and harmful. Chemicals may be used to stimulate the human body to excrete dangerous *radioisotopes.* Experiments have shown that radioactive PLUTONIUM in bones or the liver may be displaced by harmless materials. R.C.S./M.K.H.

SEE ALSO: NUCLEAR REACTORS; NUCLEAR SCIENCE; RADIATION; RADIATION, BIOLOGICAL EFFECTS OF; RADIATION, USES

Radiation, uses The dangers of radiation have been given much publicity, but there are also many beneficial uses that have become tremendously important. Radiation helps people "see" things that they can't look at normally. Powerful *gamma rays, beta rays,* and *X rays* travel through materials that stop light. Radiation and radiation detection equipment makes it possible to "see" such things as internal body organs and structures otherwise hidden by skin and other tissue.

The dangers of radiation are sometimes outweighed by likely benefits. Since radiation is active on living CELLS, it is useful in medicine. By concentrating radiation in specific areas of the human body, medical workers can often kill harmful CANCER cells while limiting damage to healthy cells. Radiation has been used to destroy bacteria and other microorganisms in packaged food. Radiation is now being used in a variety of other ways in medicine, research, and industry.

To be useful, radiation must be available where it is needed, in the quantity or intensity required, and of the types needed. Usually, such radiation is produced by a *radioisotope* (radioactive ISOTOPE) of an element. Radioisotopes are produced generally by bombarding stable nuclei with neutrons. The resulting radioactive isotope may be either the same element or a different element. Short-lived radioisotopes must be used promptly after being produced. Very high intensity radiation is available at nuclear reactors and from used fuel assemblies from reactors. *Fission* products from nuclear reactors are all radioactive. Such fission products are used to provide whatever types and quantities of radiation may be desired.

TRACERS

Tracers are radioactive atoms present along with stable atoms of the same element.

Daniel Oldfield; Argonne Hosp., U. of Chicago, USAEC

Two million electron-volt Van de Graaff generator for producing high energy X-rays for cancer therapy

Chemically, a tracer atom is identical to any of the stable atoms of the element. Therefore, the tracers go through the same chemical processes as the stable atoms. The number of tracer atoms present in a sample can be determined by measuring the radioactivity of the sample. A compound containing a tracer is said to be *labelled* with the tracer. Tracers are widely used in medicine, science, agriculture, and industry.

Tracers are helpful in research on living things. Radioisotopes are built into compounds which are foods for plants and animals, such as fertilizers and sugars, and can be traced through the life processes of the plant or animal. The use of tracers allows many types of biological activity to be studied in much more detail than was possible with radiation.

For example, iodine-131 can be used to locate problems in the human THYROID gland. A doctor gives a person suspected of having thyroid trouble a drink containing a tiny amount of iodine-131. The iodine concentrates in the thyroid gland and emits gamma rays, which are detected outside the body with a RADIATION DETECTOR. An abnormally large number of gamma rays may indicate trouble because an unhealthy thyroid gland takes up more iodine than a healthy one. *Radiocarbon* (carbon-14) and *radiophosphorus* (phosphorus-32) are similar tracers that are used with plants. Radiocarbon is used in making carbon dioxide, which is then released into airtight greenhouses. The plants pick up the radiocarbon and it moves into various tissues of the plant at different rates, depending upon the type of tissue, location, and so

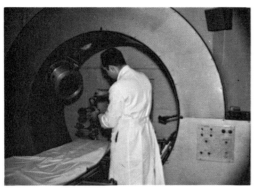

Daniel Oldfield; Argonne Hosp., U. of Chicago, USAEC

A revolving cobalt-60 generator source that emits one and one-fourth million electron-volt gamma rays is used in cancer therapy. The apparatus turns around the patient

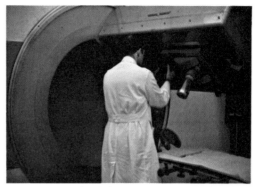

Daniel Oldfield; Argonne Hosp., U. of Chicago, USAEC

A 50 million electron-volt scanning linear accelerator, for producing a pencil beam of electrons that is moved by magnets over the area to be irradiated

on. Radiophosphorus is fed to plants in nutrient solutions that cover the plant roots.

Tracers are also used to study reaction mechanisms. For example, if the reaction to be studied is one in which one large molecule and one small molecule are formed, and if the researcher wants to know whether a particular atom in the starting substance goes into the large molecule or the small one, some of the original molecules are labelled with a tracer of the atom of interest. After the reaction, the large molecules are separated from the small ones and the radiation from each is measured. The presence of the tracer in one sample will show to which molecule the atom went.

RADIATION IN INDUSTRY

Radiation has a number of uses in industry. Manufacturers have used radiation to produce new types of plastic that have a much greater resistance to heat and deterioration than non-irradiated types. The ionization produced by the radiation results in a larger number of bonds between the molecules of the plastic. Some food manufacturers use radiation to preserve packaged foods, making it unnecessary to refrigerate the items. Security check points at airports use X rays to look for hidden weapons or explosives. And nuclear power plants produce heat energy in a reaction called nuclear fission, which is used to generate electricity.

RADIATION IN RESEARCH

Because radiation produces mutations, it is used to produce a great variety of hereditary changes in plants. Selections are made of the mutants which have desirable quali-

ties. Several new strains of cultivated food crops, which have a higher yield and improved resistance to disease and drought, have been developed in this manner.

Radiation is used in ARCHEOLOGY to determine the age of many ancient objects by measuring the amount of radioactive carbon the objects contain. Astronomers study the X rays, gamma rays, and cosmic rays that originate in outer space. These high energy radiations give clues about intriguing objects such as QUASARS, PULSARS, and BLACK HOLES.

RADIATION IN MEDICINE

The most common application of radiation in medicine is medical and dental X ray examinations. Physicians use X rays to make photographs of the bones and organs of the human body. A *CAT scanner* creates X ray images of organs as they function inside the body. Dentists use X rays to reveal cavities in teeth.

Dangerous cancer cells in the human body may be destroyed by radiation from suitable radioisotopes. The radioisotope may be put into a needle or pellet and implanted among the cells to be destroyed. Beams of X rays, gamma rays, or other forms of energy are often focused on malignant growths in cancer patients. By controlling the angles of the radioactive beams and the amount of exposure, cancer cells can be killed while limiting damage to healthy cells.   R.C.S./M.K.H.

SEE ALSO: ELEMENTS; NUCLEAR SCIENCE; RADIATION; RADIATION, BIOLOGICAL EFFECTS; RADIATION, PROTECTION

Radiation sickness see Radiation, biological effects of

Radical, chemical A chemical radical is a combination of two or more kinds of atoms that stay together during chemical changes. A radical, when it is not taking part in chemical change, is part of a molecule of some substance.

When in water solutions, inorganic radicals usually form *ions* (electrically-charged groups). Washing soda (Na_2CO_3, sodium carbonate) forms these ions in water: two sodium ions ($2\ Na^+$) and one carbonate ion radical (CO_3^{--}).

Simple chemical reactions show how radicals behave: when washing soda solution and limewater or $Ca(OH)_2$ are mixed, they react to form a precipitate of lime carbonate ($CaCO_3$) and caustic soda ($NaOH$). The equation is:

$$Na_2CO_3 + Ca(OH)_2 \rightarrow CaCO_3 + 2\ NaOH$$

Note that the carbonate (CO_3^{--}) and hydroxide (OH^-) radicals each remain as undivided groups of atoms despite the change in their combinations with sodium (Na) and calcium (Ca) atoms.　　　D. A. B.

SEE ALSO: CHEMISTRY

Radicle (RADD-ick-uhl) As a seed grows, it forms a young plant. This little plant has the beginnings of a root, stem, and leaf. This first small root growing from the seed is called the radicle. The *hypocotyl* (stem) and the *plumule* (leaves) are other parts of the embryo.

The radicle of a young seedling develops into the primary root which, in turn, sends out secondary roots. The cells in the radicle are similar in structure and function. As it matures into the primary root, the cells differentiate into tissues designed to conduct, strengthen, protect, or produce new root growth.　　　H. J. C.

SEE ALSO: GERMINATION, HYPOCOTYL, PLUMULE, SEEDS

Radicle in kernel of corn

Radio Radio is used to send and receive signals by means of electric waves without using a connecting wire. Sound waves, such as those from the human voice, are changed into information-bearing alternating voltages at the transmitting station. These are then stepped up to a higher frequency and radiated as *electromagnetic waves*. Distant receiving antennas have voltages induced into them by these waves, and the original wave patterns are "taken out" for use.

Radio is an important means of communication. Used for entertainment and for commercial public broadcasting, it would be hard to find a home in an industrialized nation that does not possess one. *Radiotelephones* use radio waves in combination with a telephone hook-up for ship-to-shore communication, and police, and taxi dispatches. RADAR uses radio waves; airplanes are kept on beam by radio waves. *Walkie-talkies* are radio sets. Television sound is a refined outgrowth of radio.

DEVELOPMENT

Many scientists in many different countries helped develop radio. JOSEPH HENRY of America and MICHAEL FARADAY of England experimented independently with *electromagnets* in the 1800's. From their researches came the understanding of the close relationship between *electricity* and *magnetism*.

Particularly useful in the development of radio was the discovery: (1) that electricity flowing in one circuit could act through space and cause (*induce*) electricity to flow in an adjacent, but unconnected circuit; (2) that a coil of wire carrying electrical current became a magnet which could attract and repel iron. Without this knowledge of electromagnetism, it would not have been possible to design circuits which can transform electrical energy into sound energy, or the reverse. The knowledge of electromagnetic induction made possible the design of transformers and oscillators—both used in radio transmission and reception.

In 1894 a young German scientist, Heinrich Hertz, showed that electrical energy was similar to light. He caused a spark to

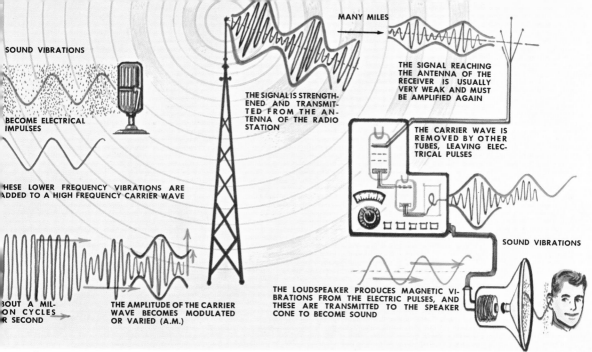

SOUND VIBRATIONS

BECOME ELECTRICAL IMPULSES

THESE LOWER FREQUENCY VIBRATIONS ARE ADDED TO A HIGH FREQUENCY CARRIER WAVE

ABOUT A MILLION CYCLES PER SECOND

THE AMPLITUDE OF THE CARRIER WAVE BECOMES MODULATED OR VARIED (A.M.)

THE SIGNAL IS STRENGTHENED AND TRANSMITTED FROM THE ANTENNA OF THE RADIO STATION

MANY MILES

THE SIGNAL REACHING THE ANTENNA OF THE RECEIVER IS USUALLY VERY WEAK AND MUST BE AMPLIFIED AGAIN

THE CARRIER WAVE IS REMOVED BY OTHER TUBES, LEAVING ELECTRICAL PULSES

THE LOUDSPEAKER PRODUCES MAGNETIC VIBRATIONS FROM THE ELECTRIC PULSES, AND THESE ARE TRANSMITTED TO THE SPEAKER CONE TO BECOME SOUND

SOUND VIBRATIONS

jump across two electrically-charged points; this spark produced electromagnetic waves that moved into space at light speed, 186,000 miles (300,000 kilometers) per second. The next year, an Italian scientist, Guglielmo Marconi, showed that such waves could be used for communication purposes. This was the first commercial use of electromagnetic waves for long-range, practical communication purposes.

In 1904 the VACUUM TUBE (more commonly now called *electron tube*) was invented. The idea was suggested by the Edison effect. In 1883 THOMAS EDISON found that electrons would flow from a glowing *cathode* to a metal plate when both the CATHODE and plate were in an evacuated envelope.

Sir John A. Fleming of England found that if he put a positive charge on the metal plate, the electron flow was greatly improved. He attempted to put this discovery into practice to improve the reception of Marconi's radio waves. He connected the *aerial* which received the waves to the plate of his tube. These *oscillating waves,* inducing an alternating voltage in the wire, made the plate alternately positive and negative. When the voltage on the plate was negative, the current did not flow. When the voltage on the plate was positive, current flowed from the cathode to the plate. Fleming called his tube a "valve" because it controlled the flow of current. Today it is called a *rectifier* because it changes alternating current into a current flowing in only one direction.

John Fleming's tube was called a *diode*

because it had but two elements, the *filament* and the *plate*. In 1907, the *triode,* or vacuum tube having a third part, the *grid,* was developed by LEE DE FOREST in the United States. Depending on the charge on it, this grid or metal screen, when inserted between the filament and plate, completely controlled the current reaching the plate. When connected to an antenna, the alternating radio frequency carrier makes the grid alternately positive and negative. When it is positive a powerful current flows in the tube circuit. The tube thus acts as an *amplifier* to strengthen the current.

Using triodes, it is possible to generate waves of a frequency high enough for radiation. If current from any ordinary storage battery is fed to a coil and capacitor combination, the current will surge back and forth within the combination. If this surging (changing current), is now fed to the grid of a triode, the plate current of the triode will alternately change back and forth. If some of the plate current is fed back into the grid circuit by electromagnetic induction, the plate current becomes even stronger. When the feedback current is strong enough to overcome the losses in the grid circuit, the tube is said to be *oscillating*. Such a circuit is an oscillator circuit.

Many different tubes have been developed for many different purposes. Most of them are further developments of the ideas first found in the diode and triode. Tubes used in certain parts of radar equipment which operates at microwave frequencies are very different from the conventional triode.

1417

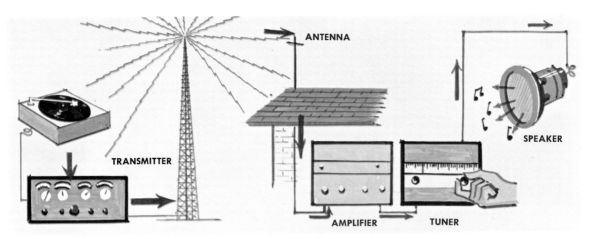

Components necessary to allow transmission and reception of sound without wires

Further refinements have been made during the mid-twentieth century, primarily through the invention of transistors. The transistor is silicon or germanium that has been doped with arsenic, phosphorous, or antimony. Transistors have almost totally replaced tubes. They are smaller, draw less current, and last longer than tubes.

HOW RADIO WORKS

Transmission: The essential parts of radio transmission, which transforms sound waves into radio waves and sends them out into space, are: (1) A *microphone* which translates sound waves into a varying electrical current in a circuit. Sound waves set the diaphragm of a microphone vibrating, which modifies the strength of an electric current so that it exactly corresponds with the vibrations set up by the sound waves. This varying *audio frequency* current then flows through *amplifying tubes* and *transformers.*

(2) A *radio-frequency generator,* which produces an alternating, high-frequency current. This current is generated by vacuum tubes or semiconductor feedback circuits and amplifiers. (3) A *modulator* which mixes the audio-frequency (low frequency) voice current with the radio-frequency (high frequency) alternating current so that the resulting current is modified or varied to conform with the voice signal. This can be done in two ways: by varying the amplitude (strength) of the radiated wave—AM or *amplitude modulation;* or by varying the frequency of the radiated wave—FM, *frequency modulation.* (4) An *antenna* into which the modulated high-frequency current is sent from which electromagnetic radio waves are launched into surrounding space.

Radio waves are classified by their frequency in alternations per second or multiples of them. One alternation per second is now called one *hertz;* 1,000 per second, one *kilohertz;* and one million per second, one *megahertz.* One such classification is:

Low frequencies (for radio navigation, government, and marine radiotelegraphy), 30 to 300 kilohertz.

Intermediate frequencies (for AM broadcasting, marine communication), 300 to 3,000 kilohertz.

High frequencies (for shortwave broadcasting, amateur communication, long-range telegraphy) 3,000 to 30,000 kilohertz.

Very high and *ultra-high frequencies* (for FM and TV broadcasting; aircraft, police, and industrial communication; radar; radio astronomy) 30,000 to 100,000 megahertz, with higher frequencies in prospect.

These electromagnetic radio waves induce a high-frequency alternating voltage when they pass a *receiving antenna.* This voltage is delivered to a *receiver.* Here *frequency selecting circuits,* consisting of inductors and capacitors, select the desired frequency. The a.c. voltage, after being amplified by vacuum tubes or semiconductors, goes to a *demodulator.* This removes the voice, music, or other information content as a voltage of lower frequency range. This is further amplified and delivered to a *loudspeaker* which converts the electrical energy into sound waves. D. A. B.

SEE ALSO: ELECTRICITY, ELECTRONICS, INDUCTION, TELEGRAPH, TELEPHONE, SOUND

Radio beacon see Beacon

Radio telescope A radio telescope is an instrument that receives radio waves from space rather than light waves as in optical telescopes. These radio waves are transmitted by various celestial bodies. Radio telescopes are enabling astronomers to discover many new facts about heavenly bodies.

The radio waves that are received by the gigantic radio telescopes are transmitted naturally. It is thought that these radio waves are produced by the action and interaction of electrons with magnetic fields or with other subatomic particles. With the use of computers and other complex devices, astronomers can analyze these natural radio signals to determine the nature of the body producing their emission.

K. J. Jansky of the Bell Telephone Laboratories was the first to detect the presence of this type of radiation. In 1931, he conducted experiments that would enable him to learn more about radio static, which he thought originated in the Earth's atmosphere. With further investigation and the construction of a large revolving antenna, he discovered new and different waves that appeared to originate in outer space. This was the beginning of the science of *radio astronomy*.

Radio telescopes have saucer-like or flat-type (also called *helical*) antennas. These antennas receive the radio waves and direct them to electronic ampliyfing and recording devices.

These cosmic radio waves that are received at the Earth's surface are very weak, so the antenna of the radio telescope must be very large. Most radio telescopes are movable, so that they can be focused or pointed at various points in the celestial sphere. Since the telescopes are so large, they require huge machinery to turn them. Recently some radio telescopes have been built into natural or man-made depressions on the surface of the Earth. These telescopes are tremendous in size and can receive radio signals from great distances. Since this type is not "steerable," it depends upon the Earth's movement to focus on the various areas of the celestial sphere.

The *paraboloidal* or "dish" type of radio telescope is in wide use by astronomers today. It focuses the incoming radio waves on a *dipole* which extends outward from the center of the antenna. These waves are then picked up by the dipole, where they are changed into measurable electric voltage. The signals from them are then amplified and recorded.

Radio telescopes have the advantage of being effective in both daylight and darkness.

H. S. G.

SEE ALSO: ASTRONOMY, INTERSTELLAR COMMUNICATION, TELESCOPE

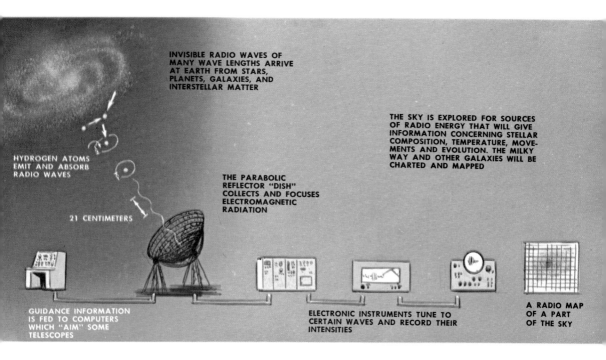

INVISIBLE RADIO WAVES OF MANY WAVE LENGTHS ARRIVE AT EARTH FROM STARS, PLANETS, GALAXIES, AND INTERSTELLAR MATTER

THE SKY IS EXPLORED FOR SOURCES OF RADIO ENERGY THAT WILL GIVE INFORMATION CONCERNING STELLAR COMPOSITION, TEMPERATURE, MOVEMENTS AND EVOLUTION. THE MILKY WAY AND OTHER GALAXIES WILL BE CHARTED AND MAPPED

HYDROGEN ATOMS EMIT AND ABSORB RADIO WAVES

THE PARABOLIC REFLECTOR "DISH" COLLECTS AND FOCUSES ELECTROMAGNETIC RADIATION

21 CENTIMETERS

GUIDANCE INFORMATION IS FED TO COMPUTERS WHICH "AIM" SOME TELESCOPES

ELECTRONIC INSTRUMENTS TUNE TO CERTAIN WAVES AND RECORD THEIR INTENSITIES

A RADIO MAP OF A PART OF THE SKY

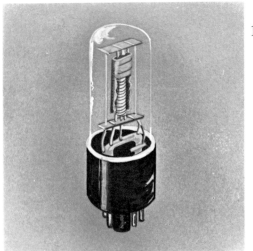

A radio tube is the heart of radio

Radio tube A radio tube is a device used in older radio and television receivers to change an electric signal (current). The tubes used in the transmitters, which send out signals, are similar to radio tubes but are much larger.

Most radios and televisions today use solid-state (semiconductor) electronics. Radio tubes are among the components that have largely been rendered obsolete by these solid-state devices. The newer solid-state components are smaller than comparably performing radio tubes, generate less heat, are less costly, and respond more quickly.

The simplest radio tube is the *diode*. It consists of a CATHODE and a plate (ANODE) in a highly evacuated glass or metal envelope (bulb). When the cathode is heated it emits electrons. If a positive voltage is placed on the plate, the electrons are attracted by the plate. If a negative voltage is placed on the plate, the electrons are repelled by the charge on the plate. The diode thus can be used as a *rectifier* to change alternating current into direct current.

When a grid of wires is placed between the cathode and the plate, a small change in voltage on the grid can cause a large change in the amount of current reaching the plate. Thus the *triode* can be used as an *amplifier*.

C.L.K.

SEE ALSO: ELECTRICITY, RADIO

Radio wave see Electromagnetic spectrum, Radio

Radioactive decay see Nuclear science

Radioactive elements In comparison to the number of artificially radioactive ELEMENTS there are only a few which are naturally radioactive. Two of the most important of the natural ones are *uranium* and *radium*.

Three distinct series of radioactive elements occur in nature. These are the *uranium-radium series*, the *thorium series,* and the *actinium series*. All the elements in these series are produced by the disintegration of a parent element. The most important of the three is the uranium-radium series.

Henri Becquerel, in 1896, investigated a new form of RADIATION. He found that uranium salts emitted rays similar to those described by WILHELM ROENTGEN in earlier experiments. Becquerel discovered that the decay of uranium was an inherent property of the material itself, and that it was not initiated by any outside influence.

Shortly after Becquerel's discovery, Madame Marie Curie, working in Paris, began an intense investigation of the phenomena exhibited by URANIUM. Instead of uranium, however, she used *pitchblende* ore which was about 70 to 75 per cent uranium oxide. She found that the ore was three or four times as active as the amount of uranium present could account for. In 1898, she and her husband, Pierre Curie, announced the discovery of a new and more powerful radioactive substance called *polonium*. Later in that same year came their discovery of the extremely radioactive substance, *radium*.

The availability of these new elements gave other experimenters the necessary materials with which to carry out further investigations. In 1902, Rutherford and Soddy found that radioactivity in elements was produced by *spontaneous decay* of the atom. Also, when the atom did decay, definite fractions of the total mass of the atom were emitted.

According to theory, some of these disintegrations result in a decrease in atomic weight of 4. These are attributed to *alpha particle emission*. The other disintegrations involve very little change in mass. These are caused by *beta particle emission,* along with *gamma rays*. Although beta particles produce little change in mass, they do change the chemical nature of the ATOM.

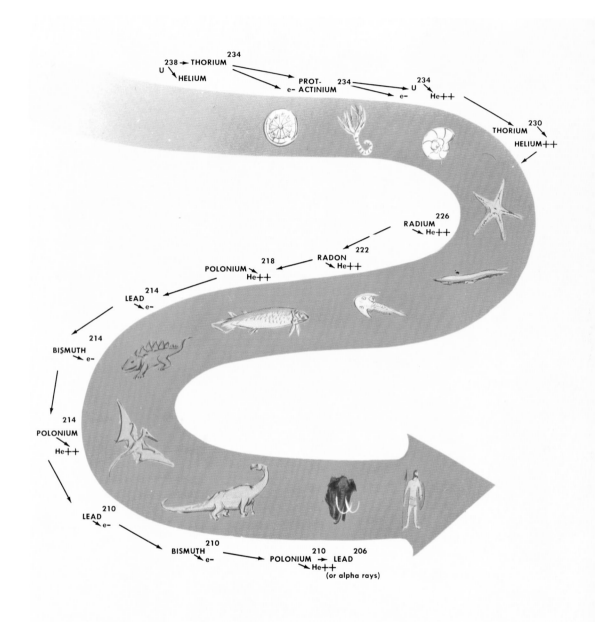

CHANGES FROM ONE ELEMENT TO SIMPLER ONES HAPPEN AT A FIXED RATE. IT TAKES 4½ BILLION YEARS FOR HALF OF ANY ORIGINAL AMOUNT OF U-238 TO CHANGE ALL THE WAY TO LEAD (Pb)

The rate at which these radioactive elements "wear out" or decay is quite important. It takes about 1600 years for a mass of radium to lose half of its original activity. An expression may be derived for the amount of time it takes for a certain element to lose half of its original activity (HALF-LIFE). The derivation is quite involved, so only the end result will be given here:

$$T = \frac{\log_e 2}{\lambda}$$

T is called the HALF LIFE of the element and λ (lambda) is the decay constant for that particular element. Some elements have a half life of only .000001 second.   A. E. L.

Radioactive fallout see Fallout; Radiation, biological effects of

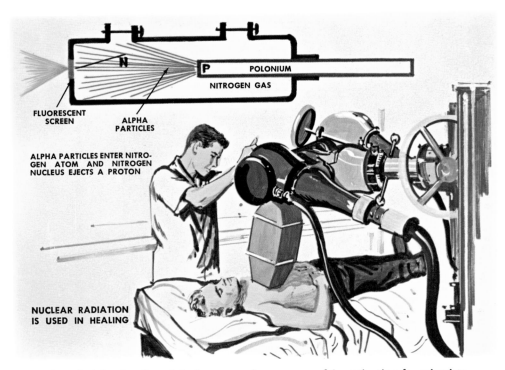

FLUORESCENT
SCREEN

ALPHA
PARTICLES

N

P POLONIUM

NITROGEN GAS

ALPHA PARTICLES ENTER NITRO-
GEN ATOM AND NITROGEN
NUCLEUS EJECTS A PROTON

NUCLEAR RADIATION
IS USED IN HEALING

The principle of radioactivity has opened vast areas of investigation for scientists

Radioactivity The discovery of radium was followed by André Debierné's discovery of *actinium* in 1899. With two RADIOACTIVE ELEMENTS known a whole new period of research began. Among the most successful experimenters were Marie and Pierre Curie. They discovered polonium and radium. Ernest Rutherford and Frederick Soddy developed the theory of disintegration of radioactive elements.

The rays emitted by these substances were soon found to be of a more complex nature than they were first thought to be. In the presence of a *magnetic field* perpendicular to the path of the rays, some of the rays bent to the right, others to the left, and still others could not be deflected from their paths at all. Further investigation showed that those which could be bent most easily were negatively charged; the less easily bent were positively charged; and those which could not be bent carried no charge whatsoever. The negative rays are known as *beta particles* (electrons); the positive rays are called *alpha particles;* and those carrying no charge are called *gamma rays.*

An important physical property of a radioactive material is a warmer temperature than its surroundings. This is due to the stoppage of the particles by the substance which emits them. The alpha particles account for most of the increase in temperature because they have a much greater energy than the other particles. About nine-tenths of the total energy of radium is due to alpha particles, while the remaining energy is due to beta particles and gamma rays.

Another important physical property of radioactive substances is their ability to cause certain other materials to *fluoresce* or *phosphoresce*. A substance called *zinc blende* is very sensitive to alpha particles, and screens coated with this material will show even, minute light flashes (*scintillations*) wherever they are struck by decay particles. Zinc blende, along with radium, is a favorite substance for making *luminous paints* seen on road and advertising signs.

The chemical reactions and physiological effects of radioactivity can be both harmful and helpful. Chemically, radiation can decompose water, *oxidize* certain materials, and produce contrast on a photographic plate much in the same manner as light. Beta particles and gamma rays are the most effective in a physiological sense, due to their greater power of penetration. They can destroy both harmful and good bacteria as well as the cells of higher plants and animals. One use of this property is in the treatment of certain types of cancer and other tumorous growths in the human body.

As was mentioned earlier, the three main decay particles of radioactive elements are beta particles, alpha particles, and gamma rays. Alpha particles were soon discovered to be positively charged nuclei of *helium.*

In 1903 Sir William Ramsay and Soddy found the atomic weight of an alpha particle to be four, and its identity as a helium nucleus was definitely confirmed at the same time. These particles are very powerful ionizers of gas.

The rays which were more easily bent, the beta particles, were shown to be electrons traveling at a very high speed. Beta particles have a very wide range of velocities ranging anywhere from zero to 99.8 per cent of the *velocity of light,* which is 3×10^{10} cm/sec. The velocity attained by accelerating an electron through 80,000 volts is only about one-half the velocity of light. With 8 million volts the electron will duplicate the velocity of the fastest beta particle. To bring electrons to greater speeds, huge *magnetic coils* and heavy *insulation* are needed; hence the enormous size of the various *particle accelerators* in existence today. The electrons can then be aimed at a target for practical application.

As a result of the high speed and small mass of the beta particle, it has much more penetrating power than the alpha particle.

The gamma rays are similar to X-RAY except that they have a shorter wave length and higher penetrating power. They can pass through a block of lead 10 inches (25.4 centimeters) thick; X rays are stopped by a few tenths of an inch of lead. Gamma rays are generally emitted at the same time as beta particles, and both are known to come from the nucleus of the atom.   A.E.L.

SEE ALSO: ACCELERATORS (PARTICLE); CURIE, PIERRE AND MARIE; NUCLEAR ENERGY; NUCLEAR SCIENCE; RADIATION; RADIUM

Radioastronomy see Astronomy, Radio telescope

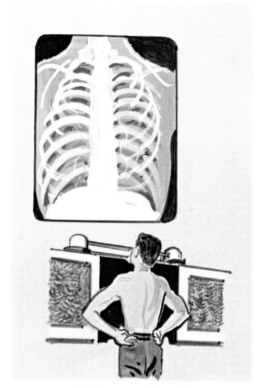
Making a radiograph

Radiograph A radiograph is a photograph produced on a film or a plate by X-rays or gamma rays instead of by light rays. The rays pass through the object being photographed. The object absorbs the rays depending upon its nature and thickness. The resulting photograph is a shadow picture. Photographic films are sensitive to X-RAYS and gamma rays. WILHELM ROENTGEN made the first radiographs in 1896.

Radiographs are useful in medicine and dentistry. In industry, solid objects, such as castings and welds, are examined by making radiographs of the objects. In X-ray diffraction, radiographs are used to analyze the atomic and molecular structures of substances. In gamma radiography, rays from radium are used to make radiographs of solid objects.   D. A. B.

SEE ALSO: PHOTOGRAPHY; RAY, GAMMA

Radioisotopes see Radiation

Radiolaria see Protozoa

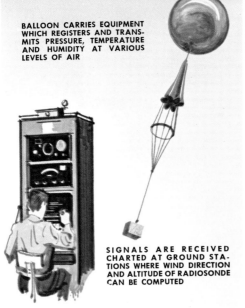

BALLOON CARRIES EQUIPMENT WHICH REGISTERS AND TRANSMITS PRESSURE, TEMPERATURE AND HUMIDITY AT VARIOUS LEVELS OF AIR

SIGNALS ARE RECEIVED CHARTED AT GROUND STATIONS WHERE WIND DIRECTION AND ALTITUDE OF RADIOSONDE CAN BE COMPUTED

Radiosonde helps increase our knowledge of upper atmosphere and weather.

Radiosonde (RAY-dee-o-zond) Radiosonde is one of the tools of the weathermen. A balloon carries a tiny RADIO set into the upper air. A receiving set on the ground picks up signals from the *transmitter* in the balloon. The signals give information about temperature, pressure, and humidity in the upper ATMOSPHERE. By tracking the soaring balloon with RADAR, weathermen can also learn about the direction and speed of the wind.

The balloons used in radiosonde are filled with HELIUM, a gas which is lighter than air. Helium is the gas used in the balloons that are sold at circuses, fairs, and big parades. Radiosonde balloons are larger and stronger than those the balloon man sells. But, like them, when the radiosonde balloon is released, it soars far up into the atmosphere.

The balloon carries lightweight weather instruments and a miniature shortwave transmitter. The weather instruments include a small *thermometer* made of a bimetallic strip, a metal *aneroid barometer,* and a metal-coated device which measures *humidity* by variations in its electrical resistance. These measurements are automatically converted to electrical impulses and transmitted by the shortwave set. The shortwave set broadcasts its signals over a special frequency to the ground receiver.

The United States Weather Bureau sends up radiosonde balloons twice a day. They can go as high as 100,000 feet (30,480 meters). Similar to radiosonde is the *dropsonde*. The dropsonde is carried into the upper air by airplanes. Similar equipment is attached to a parachute and dropped from the plane at 20,000 to 30,000 feet (6,096 to 9,144 meters).   C.L.K.

SEE ALSO: WEATHER FORECASTING

Radiotherapy see Radiation, uses of

Radish The radish is a plant related to *mustard*. The large root is usually eaten raw as a relish or in salads. It has little food value but is decorative and has a biting taste.

The small red and pink varieties that are round or oblong are the most common. The winter or Chinese radish grows to a large size and is black or white in color. It can be stored through the winter and is often boiled and eaten like turnips.

The rat-tail radish does not have an enlarged root but is grown for its long seed pods. The pods are pickled or eaten raw in salads.

Radishes were grown in China over 1,000 years ago. Today, they are grown all over Europe, Asia, and North America.   J. M. C.

radishes

Radium (RAY-de-um) Radium is ELEMENT 88 in MENDELEEV'S PERIODIC TABLE. It is radioactive and it gives off *alpha, beta,* and *gamma* RAYS. The Curies discovered radium in 1898. The oxidation number (*valence*) of radium is two.

Without any other influences, radium will change into certain other elements by radioactive decay.

Radium itself, as it is found in the

earth's crust, is a product of the decay of another element—*uranium.* Most of radium's uses are in the medical field.

Today radium is produced and used in the form of salts, such as radium *chloride,* radium *bromide,* and radium *carbonate.* Radium is in the same family of elements as *barium, strontium,* and *calcium* (alkaline earths) and has properties similar to barium except for its radioactivity.

The mass number of Ra is about 226. It has 16 ISOTOPES with mass numbers ranging from 213 to 230. It is an alkaline metal.

The crystalline salts of radium are luminous in the dark and actually give off heat, maintaining a temperature higher than their surroundings. Because the *gamma rays* given off by these radioactive salts are destructive to human tissue, they are used for the treatment of tumors in man. Overexposure to these rays, however, can cause tumors or cancers very much like the ones which can be treated. Another use of radium salts also depends upon their radioactivity, since luminous paints incorporate radium chloride for their effect.   M.S.

SEE ALSO: CURIE, PIERRE AND MARIE; ELEMENTS; RAY, GAMMA

Radius see Skeleton

Radon (RAY-dahn) Radon (symbol Rn) is *radioactive* ELEMENT 86 in MENDELEEV'S PERIODIC TABLE. It has 20 ISOTOPES. It is the heaviest of the inert gases. *Thoron* and *actinon* are its natural isotopes.

Radon is formed when RADIUM disintegrates, emitting alpha particles from its nucleus. Radon itself disintegrates, forming radium A. Radon's most stable isotope has a mass number of 222.

Radon was discovered in the radioactive transformation of radium by F. E. Dorn in 1900. It can be collected by bubbling air through a radium salt solution.

It is found in soil and rocks where it is largely trapped in minerals. Some seeps out and is detected in surface water and the atmosphere near the ground.   E. R. B

SEE ALSO: ELEMENTS, RADIOACTIVE ELEMENTS

Raffia Raffia is a fiber made from the outer layer of the leaf of an African palm tree. It is used for tying up and wrapping plants and for basket weaving.

SEE: PALM

James P. Rowan
Ragweed plant

Ragweed Ragweed is a *weed* that makes some people sneeze. In late summer, the wind blows yellow POLLEN from the plant into the air. People who are sensitive to the pollen grains are made uncomfortable or ill by breathing them.

The common ragweed plant grows to 6 feet (1.8 meters) high and has many branches and a very deep root system. The thin, somewhat lacy leaves grow on a hairy stem. The flowers containing the pollen bloom from July through October. Ragweed is a native of North America, and is found from Nova Scotia to Florida and west to Mexico. The seeds are a winter food for grouse, quail, and wild turkeys.

Giant ragweed can be 18 feet (5.5 meters), and grows some leaves over a foot (.3 meter) wide. It is usually found in rich, wet lowlands, while common ragweed grows in drier uplands. Giant ragweed is also known as *buffalo weed, horse cane,* or *wild hemp.*   P.G.B.

SEE ALSO: ALLERGY, WEED CONTROL

Rain see Precipitation, Rain making, Weather

HOW MUCH RAIN FELL TODAY?

1 inch = 2.5 centimeters

1   If you want to determine the exact amount of rainfall in your own backyard, you will need a gauge to measure it. The weatherman's report is an average over a larger area of land.

2   Use a metal or plastic funnel the same diameter as any wide-mouthed jar available. Since the rainfall is so slight sometimes it is difficult to measure the water collected in a large container. So figure out the same quantity in a narrow bottle. Put an inch of water into the large jar. Measure it with a ruler. Now pour this into a tall thin bottle which is the same diameter the whole length of the bottle. Make a mark at the water level. Mark this inch into 8 equal parts. Do the same for the second and third inch.

3   Set the funnel in the large jar out in the open area away from trees and other obstructions. Immediately following a rainstorm bring the jar in and pour it into the tall measuring gauge. This enables you to read fractions of an inch.

Rain gauge A rain gauge is an instrument used to measure rainfall. Gauges measure in inches and hundredths of an inch. Metric rain gauges measure rainfall in millimeters and centimeters. Snowfall is collected in a special device, melted down, poured into the rain gauge, and read as an equivalent amount of rainfall.

In a rain gauge, a metal funnel channels the rain into a smaller cylindrical tube. The mouth of the funnel has exactly ten times the area of the mouth of the tube. The tube, therefore, will register an amount ten times greater than that which fell into the funnel. The larger amount is easier to read and must be divided by ten to determine actual rainfall.   H.S.G.

Rain making Rain making is a process which has been developed by scientists to attempt to cause rain to fall in regions needing moisture. It is important for agriculture, drinking water reservoirs, or forests in danger of fire because of dryness.

Many primitive peoples attempted to bring needed rainfall by dances and other rites. These did not influence the falling of rain, which is a physical process determined by several natural factors. Basically, in an area over which rain is to be "made," water in gaseous form (*water vapor*) must be present, and in sufficient quantities so it can be *condensed* from the *atmosphere* as rain. If there is not enough vapor, no amount of rain-making activity can succeed.

In order for precipitation to occur, it is necessary that CONDENSATION be brought about. There are several ways in which condensation may be caused to occur in the atmosphere. The most effective way is to bring about cooling in some manner. In Nature, this most often occurs when air is forced to rise by various causes.

Rainmaking requires the natural formation of clouds followed by artificial cooling. Either *silver iodide crystals* or solid *carbon dioxide* (dry ice) is introduced into the region of clouds. These compounds bring about cooling within the cloud. If the cooling is great enough, rain may result. The placement of the compound in the clouds is called *cloud seeding* and is most often done from an airplane. The airplane flies over the clouds, dropping the compound into them.

WHEN CAN YOU SEE A RAINBOW?

1 Rainbows can be made by holding a prism in the sunlight and letting the rays hit a white wall. Sun hitting an aquarium will cast the rainbow on the opposite side. A glass of water on a window sill will direct the sun rays into a spectrum on the inside.

2 The most effective and realistic way to make a rainbow is to take a water hose into the back yard in early morning or late afternoon. With your back to the sun shoot the water into a dark background such as a building or clump of trees. The water drops will reflect the light and break it up into the color spectrum.

Although rain making has been successful, it is not possible to absolutely "pinpoint" a rainstorm. For example, *humidity* must be present. In addition, *wind currents,* changes in air *temperature,* and other phenomena may alter the situation abruptly.

There are advantages to being able to control the atmosphere by bringing about rainfall where and when needed. As progress in this field advances, areas with irregular rainfall can look forward to enough natural precipitation to restore productivity to the soil. So far, rain making has had only limited success in local areas.   D. J. I.

SEE ALSO: CLOUDS, WEATHER

Rainbow A rainbow is a pattern of colors seen whenever *light* strikes droplets or sprays of water at the proper angle. Waterfalls and garden sprays as well as raindrops produce rainbows. Under special conditions even moonlight will bring about a rainbow.

To see a rainbow, one must stand with his back to the sun and look at the part of the sky in which the water droplets are occurring. There may be one or two rainbows. In the case of two, the colors will be in reverse order. A second rainbow occurs because of light reflections.

A rainbow results because the droplets of water act like a *prism* breaking the white light of the sun into seven colors, although one blends into another and fewer than seven are often seen. The light is bent, or *refracted,* as it enters the drop and is then reflected one or more times on interior surfaces of the drop. It finally leaves the drop, again being refracted as it enters the air, separating the white light into its colors from violet to red. When the sun is higher in the sky, the bow will be lower.   D. J. I.

SEE ALSO: LIGHT, PRISM, REFRACTION

Raisin see Grape

Ram see Sheep

Ram, the see Aries

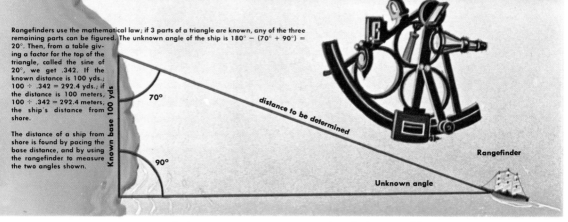

Range finders are convenient measuring devices used by man

Ramie (RAMM-ee) Ramie is a shrub that belongs to the *nettle* family. It has many stems which may grow as high as 8 feet (2.4 meters). They are about 1 inch (2.5 centimeters) thick at the base, but they become very thin and look like tall grass. A common name for ramie is *China grass.* It grows mainly in China, but also in other places where the weather is warm and moist. Egypt and India have produced this plant for thousands of years. It is used chiefly in making cloth. Egyptian mummies were wrapped in cloth made from ramie fibers.

Ramie fibers, 1 foot (.3 meter) long, are 8 times stronger than cotton fibers, and are better than those made from hemp, flax, or jute. They become stronger when wet, and will resist *mildew.* Though the stem, from which the fibers are made, becomes fuzzy and loses its beautiful white luster when it is spun, the *yarn* produced is very strong. Many companies have experimented with using ramie fibers for *textile making,* but because gums cling to them, an efficient way of cleaning them by machinery has not been found. When the slow process of cleaning the fibers by hand has been replaced by mechanization, ramie may become a popular textile fiber.   D. E. Z.

Ramjet see Jet propulsion

Range finder A range finder is an OPTICAL INSTRUMENT, used in gunnery and photography, which measures distance to a target point. The target is sighted from two places in the instrument, and the distance is figured using the difference in direction of the two lines of sight.

Raoult's Law Raoult's Law is a law of physical chemistry dealing with *solutions.* This law relates the *vapor pressure* of the solvent in a solution with the *amount* of solvent in the solution. The simple equation is as follows:

$$P_A = P_A^0 N_A$$

where P_A, the vapor pressure of the solvent in a solution, is equal to P_A^0, the vapor pressure of the pure solvent multiplied by N_A, the mole fraction of solvent in the solution. N_A is the number of moles of solvent divided by the total number of moles of solvent plus solute.

For Raoult's law to be of use for mixtures of liquids, certain rules must be obeyed by the solution. (1) The solution must contain liquids which are completely soluble or *miscible* in each other, such as alcohol and water. (2) The liquids in this mixture must be *volatile* so that they will always have a vapor pressure.

From Raoult's law comes one of the most important scientific principles regarding solutions: that of the lowering of the vapor pressure and its effect on the boiling and

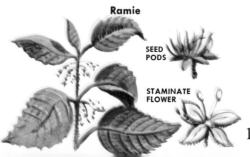

Ramie

SEED PODS

STAMINATE FLOWER

freezing points of solutions. When some non-volatile material is dissolved in a solvent, the resulting solution will have a lower vapor pressure than the solvent itself.

This is true because the water must contribute all of the vapor pressure for a solution where it is only a percentage of the whole. The higher the vapor pressure of a substance the more volatile it is and the more easily it boils. Therefore, if the vapor pressure is lowered, more energy in the form of heat or higher temperature is required for a solution to boil.

The lowering of vapor pressure by the addition of certain substances to liquids, such as salt to water, also lowers the freezing point. Salt will actually lower the FREEZING POINT of ice so that it melts on the street in the winter time. Adding alcohol or ethylene glycol ANTIFREEZE to the water in a car radiator prevents freezing by lowering the freezing point of the water from 32° F. (0° C.) to as low as -40° F. (-40° C.).   M.S.
SEE ALSO: GAS, SOLUBILITY, SOLUTIONS, SOLVENT, VAPOR PRESSURE

Rapid A rapid occurs when a section of a river suddenly begins to flow faster than the sections just above or below it. Large boulders and *whirlpools* are often present in the turbulent waters of a rapid.

A *waterfall* and a rapid are closely related. They are caused by erosion that proceeds at different rates along the course of a river. Both form around resistant rock. The slope of the resistant rock governs the force and lifetime of a rapid and waterfall. The rapids of the Colorado River in the Grand Canyon and those of the Snake River are well-known.   P.P.S.

Raptures of the deep "Raptures of the deep" is a term given to one of several serious dangers of skin diving. It appears to be related to another hazard,

Rapids flow faster than other parts of rivers.

James P. Rowan

caisson disease, called the BENDS.

When divers go too deep, they sometimes experience strange feelings. They may become drowsy and want to go to sleep in the deep water. Others may feel excitement, and want to cavort among the fish or play "games" with them. In either case they do not want to come back up to the surface.

The causes of raptures of the deep are not clearly understood, although experts have studied the condition very carefully. The air breathed is approximately four-fifths nitrogen. Under normal atmospheric conditions most of it is quickly exhaled. Under very great pressure, however, some of it seeps from the lungs into other parts of the body.

When the pressure of water surrounding the body is rapidly lowered, the nitrogen trapped in the blood and the surrounding tissues escapes too quickly, like the "fizz" in a bottle of carbonated beverage when the cap is suddenly pulled off. This causes severe pain, and results in the bends. Under continuing great pressure the nitrogen cannot escape at all and remains in the body. It is believed that this gas then attacks the nervous system, some of it seeping into the brain, causing intoxication. It is this intoxication which gives rise to the strange and dangerous *phantasies* of playfulness or drowsiness and the inclination not to return to the surface.

Numerous drownings have occurred because nitrogen *narcosis,* or raptures of the deep, was not understood. Inexperienced or untrained skin divers should never dive more than a few feet deep until they have learned to recognize, and to take preventive measures against, such dangers.   R. N. J.
SEE ALSO: OCEANOGRAPHY

Rare-earth elements The rare-earth elements, also called *lanthanides,* are a group of METALS which occur in various rare minerals. They include elements with atomic numbers 57 through 71. They have similar properties because their outer electrons are arranged the same way.
SEE: ELEMENTS

Rarefaction (RAR-uh-fak-shuhn) Rarefaction occurs to a given volume of gas (including air) when some of it is forcibly pumped out of its enclosing space or when the space is enlarged. The rarefied gas exerts less pressure. SEE: ALTITUDE, ATMOSPHERE, GAS, REFRIGERATION

Rarefied air When a person in an aircraft goes higher and higher above the surface of the earth, he gradually moves into air that is less and less dense. At high altitudes the particles of air are spread farther apart than at the surface, or *rarefied*.

Rarefied air raises certain problems not met in the denser atmosphere near the earth. There is too little air for easy breathing. The pressure of this thin air is not enough to balance the internal bodily gas pressures, and thus BENDS may result. Rarefied air offers less support, and also less resistance to high flying aircraft. Their great speeds, however, have created new problems of heating from air friction.   D. A. B.
SEE ALSO: AIR PRESSURE, ASTRONAUT, ATMOSPHERE

Raspberry The FRUIT of this bramble-bush may be red, black, white, or purple. FLOWERS are small and greenish-white. Several leaflets make up a single leaf. The leaflet edges are jagged or saw-toothed. Stems are woody with prickly thorns or spines.

Raspberry bushes have PERENNIAL roots but BIENNAL stems. A bush may be 6 feet (1.8 meters) high, but the stems are 12 feet (3.7 meters) long. After a period of upward

Red raspberry leaf and fruit

growth, they bend over and grow downward. Certain kinds PROPAGATE when the cane tips touch the ground. They take root and start a new plant. Other species propagate from root suckers.

The red raspberry has pinnately compound LEAVES of three to seven leaflets. Black raspberry leaves are made of five leaflets arranged like a fan. Flowers have both sexes and are regular or symmetrical. Their parts are in numbers of fives. The raspberry fruit is not a true berry. It is an aggregate of drupelets. Each of the several carpels of the ovary matures into a little drupe. These drupes form the hollow shells which separate from the flower stalk when the fruit is ripe.

Diseases of raspberries include the cane blight and crown gall. There is one virus which stunts the whole plant. Raspberry is a member of the rose or Rosaceae family.

    H. J. C.

Rat A rat is a rodent belonging to the same family as the mouse. It is larger than a mouse and has more scales on its tail. The snout is long and the skull strong.

The rice rat of South America and southern United States damages rice crops. It is also common on grasslands. It often lives near water. The wood rat lives in caves, cliffs, and forests. It builds a home 5 to 6 feet (1.5 to 1.8 meters) high out of grass and small sticks. The common house rats belong in the genus *Rattus*. They destroy property and carry diseases such as bubonic plague.

There are over 500 species of rats in the genus Rattus. These vary in size from about 5 inches (12.7 centimeters) to over a foot (30.5 centimeters) in length. Their tails are

The brown rat is a common pest

Kangaroo rat

very scaly. Hair color is in shades of brown or gray. Hair varies in coarseness and may be mixed with a spiny type.

Rats can live anywhere that man lives. There are many more rats than there are people. They not only breed rapidly but are OMNIVOROUS (will eat almost anything). This includes other rats. The most common rat is the brown or Norway rat. It breeds all year. *Gestation* (length of pregnancy) is three weeks and there are five to seven young in a litter. Under favorable conditions, one female may have twelve families a year. Young breed in two to three months.　　　　J. C. K.

SEE ALSO: RODENTIA, WHITE MOUSE

Ratio A ratio is a measure of a relation one quantity bears to another. The ratio is found by dividing one quantity by the other. Ratios are often written as $\frac{8}{3}$ or 8:3, and read "eight to three." For example, if 3 pencils cost 8¢, the ratio of the cost to the pencils is 8:3.

Rational number see Algebra

Example of a ratio

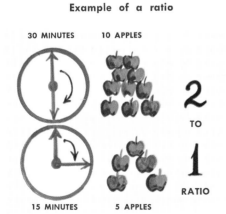

30 MINUTES　10 APPLES

2 TO 1

15 MINUTES　5 APPLES

RATIO

Rattan stems

Rattan (ruh-TAN) Rattan is a palm of tropical Asia. Many varieties have barbed tips on the leaves for climbing. The stem, noted for its flexibility and great length (up to 600 feet or 183 meters), is used to make canes, *wickerwork,* and baskets.

Rattlesnake see Snakes

Raven Ravens are very large, glossy black birds with black bills, feet, and eyes. They are often confused with another large all-black bird, the crow. However, they are almost twice the size of a crow. Ravens prey on small mammals and bird eggs.

Aside from size, there are other differences between crows and ravens. Ravens soar in flight with wings horizontal, while crows soar with wings bent upward. Throat feathers are shaggy in the raven but smooth in the crow. A raven croaks and a crow caws.

Nests are built of sticks, bits of fur, or seaweed. They lay four to seven spotted green eggs. Incubation time is three weeks long.

Ravens belong to the largest order of birds, the perching or Passerine birds. There are 69 families in the order. Crows, jays, magpies, and ravens are all in the family *Corvidae.*
　　　　J. C. K.

SEE ALSO: CROW

Raven

TORPEDO RAY

DEVIL RAY

STINGAREE

BARNDOOR
SKATE

Ray Rays are flat, disk-shaped fish in the same class as SHARKS and SKATES. They have gristle (CARTILAGE) skeletons. Pectoral fins are prolonged into triangular wings as wide as 20 feet (6.1 meters). Gills are on the undersides of the wings. Bodies, flattened from back to belly, have pointed, rat-shaped tails. In some rays, tails bear poison spines, while in others, head organs discharge electricity.

Rays and skates are often confused. Both have similarly shaped bodies. Rays swim by flapping their wings like birds, while skates move by a series of rippling waves. Electric skates have organs with electricity on their tails. Skates lay eggs, while rays give birth to living young.

Rays living on the ocean floor take in water through a spiracle on top of the head and pass it over the gills. This prevents mud from coating the gills. Rays that do not live on the bottom breathe like other fish.

Stingrays are smaller types of rays. They have more rounded, disk-shaped bodies and yellowish spots. A flattened, pointed, poisonous spine is on the dorsal surface of the stingray's tail.

Devilfish are the largest rays. They eat small crustaceans and plankton. A small pair of fins sweeps food into the mouth. They do not have poison spines or electric organs. Some are 20 feet (6.1 meters) across and weigh 1,000 pounds (454 kilograms). Females give birth to one ray.

Torpedos, or electric rays, bear electrical organs on the head. These discharge from 75 to 200 volts. Voltage decreases when the organs discharge repeatedly. Modified muscle tissue forms the electric disks making up electric organs. These disks are made of a gelatinous material with many nuclei. Several hundred disks, separated by CONNECTIVE TISSUE, are stacked in columns. There may be 150 to 1,000 columns hooked together by nerves into a parallel series. When discharging, upper surfaces are positive and lower ones negative. Only nerve stimuli cause discharge. J. C. K.

1432

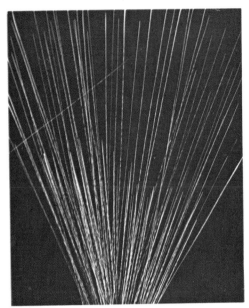 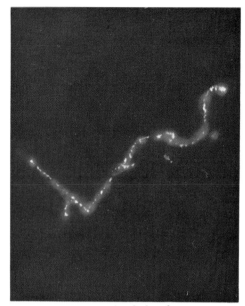

Trails of alpha rays (left) and beta particles as revealed in a cloud chamber

Ray, alpha Alpha rays are invisible, energetic particles given off by some atomic nuclei. They are charged HELIUM nuclei (He^{+2}). Some are COSMIC RAYS. Alpha rays can be dangerous. They were named after the first letter of the Greek alphabet (α) by Ernest Rutherford, a scientist who studied the rays emitted by radioactive elements.

All alpha particles from the nuclei of one particular isotope have the same velocity, unless there are two ways for the isotope to decay by emitting alphas. In that case, there would be two distinct groups of alphas, each with its own characteristic velocity. The mass of an alpha particle is about four times that of a proton.

Alpha rays travel only a few inches in air and can be stopped by a piece of paper. While they cannot penetrate the unbroken skin, they could cause considerable damage if they were freed inside the body by a *radioisotope* being used for treatment.

These rays are so small that 100 billion billion of them would be no larger than the head of a pin. When they are accelerated to high velocities, they can be used to bombard atoms in nuclear reactions.   V. B. I.
SEE ALSO: LIGHT; RADIATION; RADIATION, BIOLOGICAL EFFECTS OF; RADIOACTIVITY

Ray, beta (BAY-tuh) Beta rays are fast-moving invisible ELECTRONS given off by some radioactive NUCLEI. These nuclei decay in weak interactions. At that time, beta rays are given off. Beta rays can be dangerous. They are symbolized by the second letter of the Greek alphabet, β.

The velocities of beta rays from nuclei of one particular isotope range from zero up to a certain maximum velocity. This maximum velocity depends on the particular isotope which is decaying.

Because beta rays travel only a few feet in air, a piece of wood can stop them. But they can penetrate ⅓ of an inch (8.5 millimeters) of human tissue, causing severe burns.

Hyperthyroidism, which is caused by an overactive thyroid, has been treated successfully with beta rays. *Radioiodine* bombards the thyroid gland with beta rays. Enough cells are damaged to retard the activity of the gland.

By slowing down the activity of the thyroid gland, the rest of the body processes are also slowed down. The heart is relieved. In this way, victims of *angina pectoris,* a heart condition, may be aided to recovery.
                                        V. B. I.
SEE ALSO: LIGHT, NUCLEAR GLOSSARY; RADIATION; RADIATION, BIOLOGICAL EFFECTS OF; RADIOACTIVITY; URANIUM

PARTICLES COLLIDE WITH ATOM OF THE UPPER ATMOSPHERE TO PRODUCE OTHER PARTICLES OF LESSER ENERGY

BALLOON ASCENDS CARRYING PHOTOGRAPHIC PLATES SEALED AGAINST DAYLIGHT TO RECORD COSMIC RAYS AS THEY PENETRATE THE PACKET

FAST COSMIC RAY STRIKING HEAVY ATOM

Ray, cosmic They are invisible, penetrating, high-energy particles from space which bombard the EARTH. They are mostly PROTONS. They constantly strike upper air molecules and produce more radiations. They can easily go through a person and even through several feet of rock. The atmosphere absorbs most of these rays, yet traces of their effects have been found in water and below the ground.

Primary cosmic radiations are those outside the earth's atmosphere. They are mostly high speed *protons* or *hydrogen nuclei*. They vary greatly in energy. Helium, carbon, nitrogen, and oxygen nuclei are also found.

When these particles enter the earth's atmosphere, they *collide* with atoms, breaking the atoms up into neutrons, protons, electrons, mesons. This additional radiation is called *secondary* cosmic radiation.

Cosmic rays have been studied intensively. Scientists still are not sure where they originate. One theory says that cosmic rays were created when the universe was created; they have been traveling almost at the *speed of light,* 186,000 miles (300,000 kilometers) per second, ever since.

Another theory states that the cosmic rays are created continuously throughout our *galaxy,* the Milky Way. Those which strike the earth may come mostly from the sun. Some similarity has been noted between the intensity of cosmic radiation and activity on the sun. V.B.I.

SEE ALSO: NUCLEAR SCIENCE, SPACE

Ray, gamma Gamma rays are electromagnetic radiation of high energy, very high frequency, and great penetration. They are PHOTONS with no electric charge and no mass. In nuclear reactions alpha, beta, and gamma rays shoot out. Gamma rays have a very short wavelength. They are similar to X RAYS, but they have a higher frequency and can penetrate more deeply into matter,

Gamma rays are similar to light waves. They travel with the speed of light. The wave lengths of gamma rays, however, are much shorter than the length of light waves. In fact they are the shortest waves in the electromagnetic *spectrum.* Gamma radiations have wave lengths that vary from .0005 nanometer to .14 nanometer. Gamma rays, like X rays, are too short to be visible.

Gamma rays have a very high frequency. They can penetrate even the most densely packed materials. Gamma rays are used in ways similar to X-rays, to look into things that man cannot ordinarily see through. For example, gamma rays are used to inspect materials used in building dams, bridges, or ships to be sure there are no internal flaws in the construction. C. L. K.

SEE ALSO: NUCLEAR GLOSSARY, RADIATION

Ray, infrared It is invisible electromagnetic radiation of frequency just below red light. All bodies with temperatures above ABSOLUTE ZERO radiate some infrared ENERGY.

Infrared rays from the sun and ultraviolet lamps can be harmful to people

The long-wave infrared rays cannot penetrate window glass. When objects inside a building, however, are heated by the sun's rays, they radiate some infrared rays. That is the reason cars become extremely hot when parked in the sun during warm weather. This also explains why greenhouses are made of glass.

Sir William Herschel discovered infrared rays about 1800. Using a *prism,* he bent the rays of the sun into their component colors of red, orange, yellow, green, blue, indigo, and violet. He noticed that most of the heat came from the area outside the visible red band. He therefore concluded that this invisible radiation was similar to light except that it does not affect the eyes the same way as does light from the sun.

Infrared rays are useful in identifying molecules of certain chemicals since the frequencies of vibrations of the atoms in the molecules usually fall in the same range as the infrared rays. They are also used for invisible signaling in burglar alarms, for detection of military targets, and for missile guidance.

Doctors treat arthritis, bursitis, and other muscular pains through the application of infrared rays. V. B. I.

SEE ALSO: ELECTROMAGNETIC SPECTRUM

Ray, ultraviolet Ultraviolet rays are invisible, sometimes deadly, PHOTONS with a frequency just higher than visible violet light. Research shows they produce destructive DNA pyrimidine linkages which the body usually repairs. Most of the sun's ultraviolet rays do not reach EARTH; OZONE stops them. The ozone layer is 13 to 30 miles (20.9 to 48.3 kilometers) above Earth's surface. The temperature in the high altitudes is extremely cold; but in the ozone layer the temperature is almost as warm as it is at sea level. This is caused by ozone's absorption of ultraviolet rays.

Some ultraviolet light from the sun does reach the surface of the earth. Ultraviolet light is responsible for producing suntans and sunburns on exposed human skin. It has also been shown to produce skin CANCER and cataracts in the eye. Because the atmosphere's ozone layer is being damaged, the intensity of ultraviolet light on earth's surface is likely to increase in the near future. Sun bathers should limit their exposure to the sun to just a few minutes daily, or they should apply a strong sun-blocker.

Ultraviolet rays are used in the treatment of *acne* and other skin diseases, some forms of baldness, and some chronic ailments such as asthma. Ultraviolet lamps provide an artificial source of these rays for such treatment as well as for killing of germs in restrooms and other places where sanitation should be of primary concern. V. B. I.

SEE ALSO: LIGHT

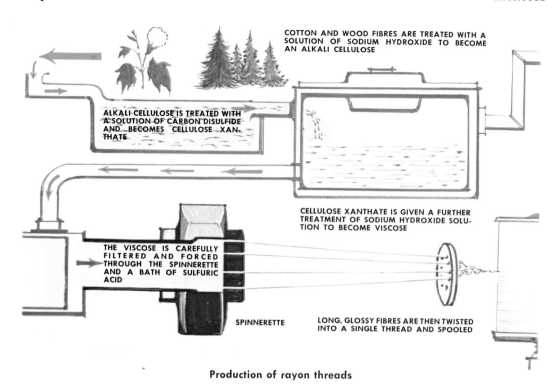

COTTON AND WOOD FIBRES ARE TREATED WITH A SOLUTION OF SODIUM HYDROXIDE TO BECOME AN ALKALI CELLULOSE

ALKALI-CELLULOSE IS TREATED WITH A SOLUTION OF CARBON DISULFIDE AND BECOMES CELLULOSE XANTHATE

CELLULOSE XANTHATE IS GIVEN A FURTHER TREATMENT OF SODIUM HYDROXIDE SOLUTION TO BECOME VISCOSE

THE VISCOSE IS CAREFULLY FILTERED AND FORCED THROUGH THE SPINNERETTE AND A BATH OF SULFURIC ACID

SPINNERETTE

LONG, GLOSSY FIBRES ARE THEN TWISTED INTO A SINGLE THREAD AND SPOOLED

Production of rayon threads

Rayon Rayon is a *fiber* made from CELLULOSE. Cellulose is a chemical compound found in the woody tissues of all plants. The Western hemlock, southern pine, and spruce, and the fibers called *cotton linters,* left on the seeds of the COTTON plant after separation of the seeds from the plant, are the sources of most of the cellulose used for making rayon in this country.

About 90 per cent of all rayon is made by the *viscose process*. Cellulose in the form of large sheets is dissolved in caustic soda and carbon disulfide. This produces a syrup the color and consistency of honey. This viscose syrup is squeezed under pressure through tiny holes in small metal cups called *spinnerets,* to form long threads or *filaments*. The filaments are hardened in an acid bath, then twisted into threads. These viscose rayon threads are almost pure cellulose. The cellulose has not been changed chemically, but simply dissolved and made into a new shape. Other kinds of rayon are made by using different *solvents* and reactions to convert the rayon to liquid form.

Rayon is made from complex organic compounds and, unlike true *synthetics* such as NYLON and orlon, is not synthesized from simple elements. In contrast to this mechanical process, the SILKWORM eats plant cellulose, and its *enzymes* change the cellulose into a protein from which it spins silk.

In 1889, Hilaire de Chardonnet, a Frenchman, first exhibited rayon, which he called artificial silk. He had made it from *nitrocellulose*. Nitrocellulose has not been used since the viscose process was discovered in 1892 in England.

Rayon has many uses. Fabrics made from rayon fibers are widely used in wearing apparel and household products such as carpets, draperies, and upholstery.

Rayon fabrics are absorbent, easily dyed, quite inexpensive, and can be handwashed or drycleaned. Stretching the filaments before they harden produces a high-tenacity fiber which is used in tire cords and industrial beltings. The *artificial textile industry* is huge, producing in recent years 2.25 million tons (2 million metric tons) of man-made fibers. The natural silk produced is only one per cent of this amount.   E.R.B.

SEE ALSO: CELLULOSE, SILKWORM, SOLVENT, SYNTHETIC FABRICS

Reaction see Chemical change, Chemistry

Reactor see Nuclear reactors

✳ **THINGS TO DO**

MAKING TWO REAGENTS FORM A PRECIPITATE

1   **Dissolve half a teaspoonful of Epsom salts (magnesium sulfate) in a test tube half full of water.**

2   **Add a little household ammonia (ammonium hydroxide), and the solu-** tion becomes white and opaque.

3   **A precipitate of magnesium hydroxide has formed. Aluminum hydroxide can be precipitated using alum and ammonia in the same way.**

Reagent (ree-AY-jennt) Reagents are chemicals used to identify other chemicals in a substance whose composition is unknown. They are also used to measure the amount of other chemicals present in a substance. A reagent is used for analysis because it always causes the same reactions with certain other chemicals—reactions which are known to the chemist.

Ammonium hydroxide is one of the common reagents found in a laboratory. It is known to cause hydroxides to precipitate out of solutions which contain certain substances.

Reagents must be pure. They are usually purified by recrystallization from solution. A saturated solution of the reagent is pre-pared in boiling distilled water. Impurities are filtered out and the solution allowed to cool. The pure reagent crystallizes out of the cooling solution.

Chemicals are available in a variety of grades. Reagent grade means they have been purified enough for ordinary chemical analysis. This is the grade used in the laboratory.

Reagents are classified on the basis of usefulness. General reagents react with many substances, such as any acid with any base. Selective ones react with a limited number of other chemicals, and specific ones react with one ion only under very limited conditions.   E. R. B.

SEE ALSO: CHEMICAL CHANGE, CHEMISTRY, PRECIPITATION, SOLUTIONS

Real image An image is a reproduction of an object formed by a lens or mirror. An image that can be projected on a screen or that is formed on a photograph is a real image.

The real image is formed by the rays of light reflected from an object coming together at a point. Real images are always upside down and vary in size.

A real image can be obtained as follows: Remove both ends of a shoe box. Cover one end of the box with thin white paper. Cover the other end with aluminum foil. Using a pin, put a hole in the middle of the aluminum foil. A burning candle in a darkened room will produce a real image on the white paper. The image of the flame is inverted and changes in size when the box is moved. A.J.H.

Real number see Algebra

Reception see Radio

Receptors Some receptors are the sense organs of taste, touch, smell, sight and hearing in an animal body. They are the structures that receive stimuli from outside the body and pass them along nerves as impulses to the brain or spinal cord. These types are called *exteroceptors*. Other receptors (*proprioceptors*) receive stimuli arising within the body. These stimuli arise from visceral organ changes such as drying of the throat.
SEE ALSO: NERVOUS SYSTEM, SENSE ORGANS

Recessive The units controlling the inheritance of such characteristics as eye color are the *genes*. Genes occur in pairs, one from each parent of the offspring. When one GENE is different from the other, the characteristic shown is that of the *dominant* gene. The other is *recessive*.
SEE: HEREDITY

Reckoning see Dead reckoning

Recording see Sound recording

Rectifier see Radio

Rectum It is the end of the *alimentary canal* or digestive system. It extends from the sigmoid colon to the anal canal—about 5 inches (12.7 centimeters) in humans. Feces accumulate in the rectum before elimination.
SEE ALSO: DIGESTIVE SYSTEM

Recycling This is a process of reusing worn out, damaged, or unwanted objects or materials. Americans produce over 75 million tons of waste each year. Because so many things are not designed for recycling, the problem of disposing worn items or items designed for one-time usage is staggering. The cost of removing and disposing of unwanted materials is around $500 million annually.

Over 80 billion bottles of drinks or food are sold each year. Dumps are filled with them. Returnable bottles present problems for the consumer and producer. Currently a dissolvable bottle is being studied.

"Tin" cans (steel containers coated with tin) decompose in 20 to 30 years. Aluminum-coated cans do not decompose, and are costly to recycle because separating the aluminum from the steel is difficult.

Thousands of automobiles are hauled to dump yards. Extracting the steel and iron is so expensive now that owners must pay to get rid of cars. They are stripped of usable parts, burned, and crushed to save space in a disposal pit. What to do with old tires is a problem, too. Only a small percentage of rubber in used tires is recycled. The newest recycling technique is heating them to extremely high temperatures to extract the oil and gas that compose the rubber.

Domestic and industrial water consumption is high. We use drinking water for everything from washing a car to flushing the toilet. Home recycling systems are rare, but it is possible to filter waste water in the

Used-up items are often discarded instead of being recycled.

California Department of Fish and Game

home and reuse it. Industrial recycling methods are also available, but laws are needed to enforce the recycling process.

Some recycling is easy to accomplish. *Composting* reuses organic wastes such as leaves, grass cuttings, food, and paper. Bacteria and fungi decompose these materials, and an excellent fertilizer and soil conditioner for gardens and lawns is formed.

Ironically, recycling can also pollute. For example, paper contains ink, bleach, and sizing. The wood pulp in the paper is reused, but the chemicals used in treating the pulp are disposed of in water and soil.

Very few communities have set up concentrated plans for sorting garbage and trash to salvage usable materials. Some techniques are the use of conveyor belts, optical sensors, grinders, and shredders. Recycling is a necessity if we are to conserve our dwindling supply of natural resources.   H.J.C.

Red adder see Snakes

Redbreast see Robin

Redbud This is the common name for the genus *Cercis* of flowering trees and shrubs. The buds, seeds, wood, bark, and FLOWERS often have a reddish col-

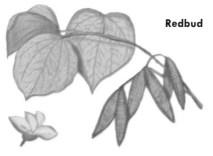

Redbud

or to them. LEAVES are heart-shaped, turning to a clear yellow in the fall.

Leaves range from 2 to 6 inches (5.1 to 15.2 centimeters) long, with long petioles, smooth margins, and palmate venation. They drop off each fall *(deciduous)*. Flowers appear in the spring, usually opening up before the leaf buds. The flowers are purplish-pink and grow in clusters, often coming out from the old bark as well as on the new branches. Each blossom is irregular, similar to a pea flower.

The FRUIT of the redbud tree is a papery legume. It is reddish purple. When this pod

is dry, it breaks open along two seams or sutures *(dehiscent)* and releases reddish-brown seeds.

Wood or lumber taken from this tree is hard, close-grained, and dark brown with a red hue. Redbud is in the pea or Leguminosae family. One redbud is also called Judas tree.

H. J. C.

Reducing agent A reducing agent is a substance which supplies the *eletrons* necessary for a reduction reaction. It is itself *oxidized* in the reaction. For example, when sodium and chlorine combine, sodium is the reducing agent because it supplies the electrons.

Reduction Reduction is a chemical reaction in which a substance loses the oxygen with which it was combined. It is the opposite of oxidation. In a broader sense reduction of a substance is any reaction in which a substance gains electrons. Reduction is often used to refine ORES.

SEE: OXIDATION, STEEL

Redwood The redwood is a gigantic, cone-bearing tree. It grows only in a narrow belt about 20 miles (32.2 kilometers) wide near the Pacific Ocean in northern California and Oregon, and near Carmel and San Francisco, California. The densest and tallest redwood forest, which also produces the finest lumber, is in northwestern California. The tree gets its name from its thick, reddish bark and wood.

Redwood trees grow to a height of about 200 feet (61 meters), though many grow to 300 feet (91.4 meters). The entire forest consists of trees of this height. They are the tallest of the fine timber trees and are also very large in diameter.

One tree can produce much fine lumber. Twenty homes, a church, a mansion, and a bank have been built from the lumber of a single redwood tree. Redwood trees live to about one thousand to fifteen hundred years old, and even older. One great redwood tree was estimated to be twenty-two hundred years old.

The redwoods are members of the genus *Sequoia*. Some sequoias are the largest and oldest living things in the world. The redwood is also known as the *ever-living* Sequoia, or *sempervierens*. The California big tree, *Sequoia gigantea,* is the only tree that has a greater diameter than the redwood; but it is not a prime timber tree.

Great fogs surround the coastal forests and over 100 inches (254 centimeters) of precipitation may fall each year. To preserve these trees for future generations, national forests have been established. M.R.L.

Reed A reed is a slender, often-jointed stem of certain tall grasses which grow in wet places. It is also the grass itself, especially the common reed of North America and Europe— a tall perennial with broad leaves which grows in ponds.
SEE: GRASSES

Reed, Walter (1851-1902) Walter Reed was the U.S. Army surgeon and bacteriologist who led the fight against the disease, YELLOW FEVER. In 1900 Dr. Reed was asked to study this disease because yellow fever was attacking many people who were building the Panama Canal.

He tested the people suffering from the disease, but found no germs in their bodies. Dr. Reed then met Dr. Carlos Finlay, who had a theory that yellow fever was caused by the bite of a mosquito. Dr. Reed bred mosquitoes and then allowed the mosquitoes to bite healthy volunteers. None of them became ill. But one of Dr. Reed's associates, Dr. James Carroll, allowed infected mosquitoes to bite him, and became severely ill with yellow fever. Another volunteer also was bitten and contracted the disease.

Dr. Reed and his associates had found the cause of the disease, the *Aedes aegypti* mosquito. By destroying the mosquito and its eggs, Dr. Reed found the way to control yellow fever. D.H.J.

Reed mace see Cattail

Coral reef Buchsbaum

Reef A reef is a build-up of rock, *coral,* and sand at the surface level of ocean water or just below it. Corals are small sea animals that live in colonies attached to the sea floor. As they reproduce, grow, and then die, their skeletal remains build up calcium deposits that help form the reef.

Living coral reefs also contain ALGAE. These simple plants provide food for coral through PHOTOSYNTHESIS and help bond together the particulate matter of the reef. Because of environmental strains, coral sometimes lose the algae living with them, often resulting in death of the colony. Coral reefs can also be damaged by heavy traps dragged across the beds of shallow ocean waters. The last living coral reefs in the U.S. are near southern Florida. H.S.G.
SEE ALSO: ATOLL, AUSTRALIA, COELENTERATA, CORAL

Refining see Metal, Petroleum, Sugar

Reflection Reflection is the bouncing or turning back of a ray of light or a sound wave from a surface. The angles the wave makes with a perpendicular to the surface as it strikes and bounces back are always equal.
SEE: LIGHT, MIRROR

Reflex action see Nervous system

Reflection from a mirror
Courtesy Society For Visual Education, Inc.

Courtesy Society For Visual Education, Inc.

Refraction in water

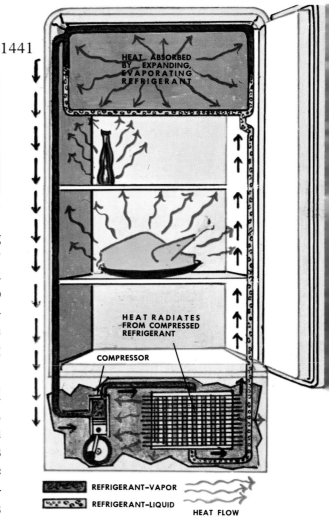

HEAT ABSORBED BY EXPANDING, EVAPORATING REFRIGERANT

HEAT RADIATES FROM COMPRESSED REFRIGERANT

COMPRESSOR

REFRIGERANT-VAPOR

REFRIGERANT-LIQUID

HEAT FLOW

Refrigeration process

Refraction Refraction is the bending or change in direction which LIGHT and sound waves undergo. When a wave goes from one kind of material to another kind where its speed is different from what it was in the first, the wave changes direction. This bending is called refraction.

Refractory Refractory is a material which will not change its weight, shape, or physical properties when subjected to high temperatures. Thus refractories are used chiefly to line furnaces, or vessels which must contain molten metal. Some refractories are fire-clay and silica.

Refrigeration Refrigeration is used to cool things for preservation. The refrigerator, freezer, and air-conditioner use the same process to cool to a different *temperature.* The freezer cools to below zero, the refrigerator to 40° F (4.4° C), and the air-conditioner to about 65° F (18.3° C).

Melting ice and evaporating liquids are the most common methods of refrigeration. A new type of refrigeration is being produced using the *thermoelectric junction device.* This has an arrangement of various materials that absorb heat at one place and give off heat at another when an electric current passes through them. Another name for this is *heat pump.* These are refrigerators because they cool by absorbing heat. Ice absorbs heat as it changes to water. Liquid will absorb heat until it reaches a temperature called the *dew point.* Then it evaporates and becomes a gas or vapor. A large amount of heat is absorbed

by a liquid when it evaporates, as is shown by evaporation of perspiration.

The principle involved in refrigeration and illustrated by the common ice box is: heat energy given to a solid can change it to a liquid. This happens when heat from the food changes solid ice to liquid water. Heat energy removed from a liquid can change it to a solid. This happens when ice is made by freezing water.

The same basic process is used in mechanical refrigerators, except that a *refrigerant* (Freon or ammonia) is changed from a liquid to a gas, instead of from a solid to a liquid.

The motor in a mechanical refrigerator drives a pump or compressor which compresses the gas. The compressed gas is then sent through a *radiator* (condenser), usually located on the back of the refrigerator. Here heat is lost. Fans sometimes drive air past the radiator to aid heat removal, or, in large installations, water is used in cooling the refrigerant. With the heat energy re-

WHICH ANIMALS CAN GROW NEW PARTS?

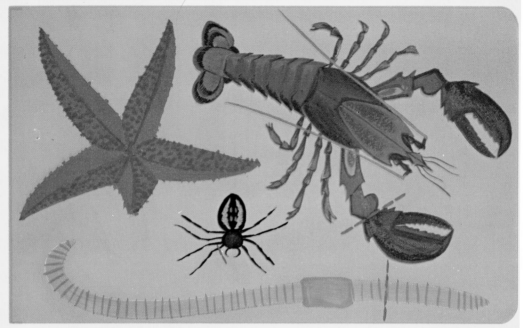

1   A variety of live animals may be collected for this experiment. Be sure to keep each one in the kind of environment it needs and supply it with adequate food and water before beginning the experiment.

2   These are the parts that can be removed without damage to the animal for it will grow a new one: the head of an earthworm, the arm of a starfish, the claw of a crayfish or a lobster, and the leg of a young spider.

3   Sponges also have great powers of regeneration. When a live sponge is pushed through a cloth mesh all the cells are separated. Soon they will clump together and grow back into a new sponge. As animals increase in complexity they lose the power of regenerating large parts of their bodies.

moved, the gas becomes a liquid and is then driven through a small pipe to the *freezer* (evaporator). Here the liquid enters larger pipes around the freezer. Heat energy taken from the food converts the liquid to a gas again. The vacuum created by the compressor assists in pulling the gas back to the compressor for re-liquefication and re-circulation.

Gas refrigerators use a flame to evaporate liquids which then are liquefied, expanding and absorbing heat in the freezer. Both types of refrigerator use thermostatic devices to control motor or flame.

Dehumidifiers use fans that draw room air over the freezer coils. The cooled air has its water vapor condensed on the coils, and then is led away. Increased use of refrigeration devices has added immensely to man's present modern comforts.   D. J. I.

SEE ALSO: AMMONIA, COMPRESSOR, HEAT BARRIER, ICE, PUMP

Regeneration Regeneration is the name given to the process by which a living thing can grow a new part of its body to replace a broken or damaged part. Some sea animals can grow a whole new body from one small part.

There are six processes involved in regeneration. The first is closure of the wound. In lower animals, surrounding tissues contract and outer cells stretch to cover the area. In higher forms blood fluids make a clot. Next, ameboid cells engulf and clear away dead cells. In addition, in higher organisms with blood tissue, dead material is broken down by enzymes (*autolysis*). In lower forms permanently undifferentiated cells (*neoblasts*) move in from surrounding areas. In complex animals, living cells in the injured area *dedifferentiate*. Following these preparatory stages, true regeneration or rebuilding begins. The neoblasts or the dedifferentiated cells

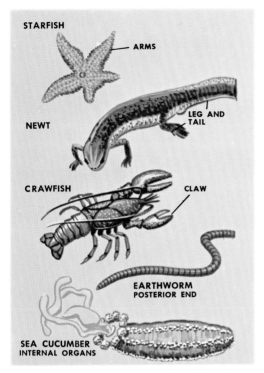

STARFISH

ARMS

NEWT

LEG AND
TAIL

CRAWFISH

CLAW

EARTHWORM
POSTERIOR END

SEA CUCUMBER
INTERNAL ORGANS

form a bud or *blastema* over the injured area. Rapid cell division provides for rapid growth. When the rate of division slows, the new cells begin to differentiate into the new structures.

Lower animals regenerate more completely from small pieces than do higher ones. For example, 1/200 of a flatworm will form a new animal. In humans, complex tissues like nerves regenerate very slowly. A severed nerve may take months or years to regenerate. If the nucleus and cytoplasm of a nerve cell are destroyed, no regeneration is possible.

J. C. K.

SEE ALSO: AUTOTOMY, MOLTING

Regulus see Constellation

Reindeer see Deer family

Reindeer moss see Lichen

Reinforced concrete Reinforced concrete is ordinary concrete which has steel rods or bars embedded in it. These increase its strength. Reinforced concrete is used when concrete parts are to be placed under extra strain.

Relapse A relapse is a return of the symptoms of a disease which occurs after the patient has begun the period of recovery of health (*convalescence*).

Relativity The theory of relativity was published by the theoretical physicist ALBERT EINSTEIN in 1905. The theory gives the laws of mechanics for objects moving at speeds approaching the speed of light. In such cases, the laws of mechanics given by Newton are no longer correct. The reason for this is because Newton's laws are based on the notion that it is always possible to determine if two events anywhere in the universe are occurring at exactly the same time. When Einstein analyzed this fundamental notion, he came to the conclusion that it was not always possible to determine "absolute simultaneity" if certain other basic laws of PHYSICS are also to hold true. These notions led to the development of the special theory of relativity.

In 1849 the speed of LIGHT was found to be 186,284 miles (299,795 kilometers) per second. Scientists supposed it needed a substance or "ether" to carry it. To see if the speed of light was different when sent out *across* the ether as compared to its speed when sent *parallel* to the ether, an experiment was conducted by Michelson and Morley.

Their experimental devices used a beam of light split into two rays: one ray was sent across the direction in which the Earth was moving in space, and the other was sent parallel to the Earth's motion. By interference, the time for both rays traveling the same distance was compared. They found no difference. Either there was no effect of "ether" or it did not exist. The results made it seem that the Earth stands still; but much other evidence already showed that the Earth moves. Scientists had no explanation that fit.

Einstein made two fundamental assumptions in developing the special theory of relativity. First, he assumed that the laws of physics must be the same for two systems

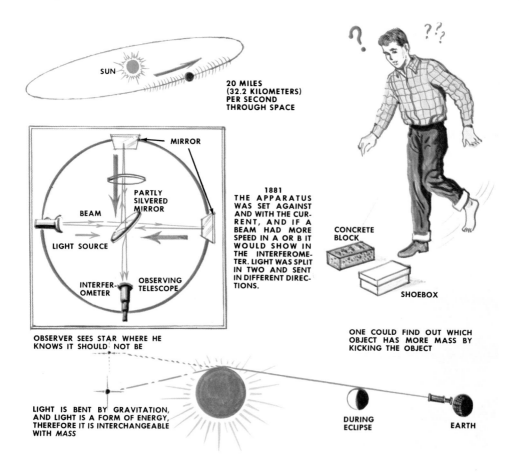

SUN

20 MILES
(32.2 KILOMETERS)
PER SECOND
THROUGH SPACE

MIRROR

PARTLY
SILVERED
MIRROR

BEAM

LIGHT SOURCE

INTERFER-
OMETER

OBSERVING
TELESCOPE

1881
THE APPARATUS
WAS SET AGAINST
AND WITH THE CUR-
RENT, AND IF A
BEAM HAD MORE
SPEED IN A OR B IT
WOULD SHOW IN
THE INTERFEROME-
TER. LIGHT WAS SPLIT
IN TWO AND SENT
IN DIFFERENT DIREC-
TIONS.

CONCRETE
BLOCK

SHOEBOX

OBSERVER SEES STAR WHERE HE
KNOWS IT SHOULD NOT BE

ONE COULD FIND OUT WHICH
OBJECT HAS MORE MASS BY
KICKING THE OBJECT

LIGHT IS BENT BY GRAVITATION,
AND LIGHT IS A FORM OF ENERGY,
THEREFORE IT IS INTERCHANGEABLE
WITH *MASS*

DURING
ECLIPSE

EARTH

that were moving relative to each other with constant velocity. Second, he assumed that the velocity of light must be the same when measured in either of the two systems. That is, the velocity of light must be independent of the motion of the source of that light.

From these assumptions, Einstein deduced that if someone measured the time it took for some event to occur in his own system, and if he then measured how long it took in another system which was moving relative to the first system, then the event would appear to take longer to occur.

Another important deduction of Einstein's was that a particle, such as an electron, that was moving would have a greater mass than the identical particle when it was standing still. This phenomenon is known as the *relativistic increase of mass*. In the design of ACCELERATORS, relativistic increase of the particles being accelerated must be allowed for, or the accelerator fails to work.

Finally, Einstein deduced the famous law of equivalence of mass and energy. Namely, a quantity of mass M is equiva-

lent to an amount of energy E, given by

$$E = Mc^2$$

where c is the velocity of light. When nuclear mass is converted to energy in an atomic explosion, this the law obeyed. The "General Theory of Relativity" presented a completely new concept of gravitation. It was viewed as a property of space rather than a force between two bodies. Since light is a form of energy, when it passes a large object such as the sun, it should experience gravitational attraction. Einstein predicted that light would bend as it neared the sun, and scientists have confirmed this during eclipses.

If one stopped in the middle of a checker game and glued all the checkers where they happened to be, those pieces remain relative to one another, but one could carry the board down on an elevator. Relative to other things the checkers change places.

Both the special theory and the general theory have been proven, without exception to be correct. Bending of light from a star, as it passes close to the sun's gravitational field, helps to prove the general theory. F. R. W.

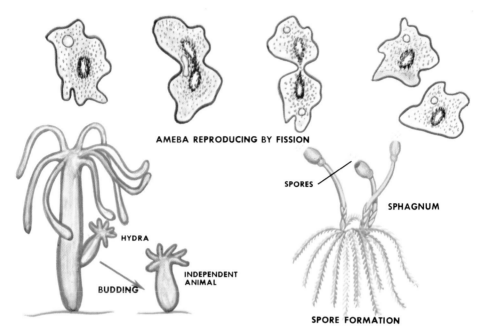

AMEBA REPRODUCING BY FISSION

HYDRA

BUDDING

INDEPENDENT ANIMAL

SPORES

SPHAGNUM

SPORE FORMATION

Reproduction, asexual (ay-SECK-shoo-uhl) Asexual reproduction is one means by which plants and animals produce offspring of their own kind. It is mostly limited to less complicated plant and animal life. In asexual reproduction only one mass of protoplasm is involved. There are four different processes of asexual reproduction.

The first and simplest type of asexual reproduction is called *fragmentation*. It is the process by which one part of a plant or animal grows and replaces the missing parts to become a whole plant or animal. A good example of an animal that reproduces by fragmentation is the *flatworm*, PLANARIA. Planaria constrict and fragment just behind the pharynx. Both pieces then develop into complete animals.

The second process of asexual reproduction is called *fission*. Fission occurs when a simple one-celled plant or animal divides into two. This method involves a kind of cell division called *mitosis*. The two "daughter" cells are exact duplicates of the one "mother" cell, meaning that the parts of the mother cell nucleus, the chromosomes, had to be duplicated before division. If this duplication of chromosomes did not take

place, the two daughter cells would only have half as many chromosomes as the mother cell. Fission occurs in the reproduction of the PROTOZOA, some algae, and most bacteria.

Another process is called *budding*. This does not have anything to do with the buds that later become flowers. In this case a new offspring simply grows from a mother plant or animal; and when it is mature enough to shift for itself, it breaks off and later becomes an independent plant or animal. This process takes place in yeast plants, in an animal called hydra, and in sponges.

The last process of asexual reproduction is called *spore formation*. The spores are usually one-celled spherical bits of protoplasm with hard outer walls. They are formed by the process of cell division by mitosis; and, therefore, each spore is capable of becoming a new plant or animal when it is set free. Spores are microscopic, and are present in the air at all times. Mosses and higher plants have a highly specialized kind of spore or gamete production involving alternation of sexual and asexual generations. Plants and the few animals that reproduce by simple spores include yeast plants, some kinds of protozoa, and many kinds of molds and bacteria. E. Y. K.

SEE ALSO: ALGAE, AMEBA, CHROMOSOME, ECHINODERMATA, FISSION, HYDRA, MITOSIS AND MEIOSIS, SPORE FORMATION, STARFISH

Reproduction, sexual In the common form of sexual reproduction, two separate parents, a male and a female, are needed to form a new living organism. Many plants, most vertebrates (frogs, fish, birds, and mammals), and many invertebrates (clams, crayfish, some snails), and many insects form their young by this kind of sexual reproduction.

Each parent produces special kinds of cells. The male parent forms SPERM cells, and the female forms EGG cells. These cells unite by a process called *fertilization* and form one cell known as a *zygote*. The zygote grows into a new animal or plant.

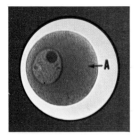

The fertilized egg, or zygote, is made up of an egg from the female parent and a sperm from the male

Photo-micrographs by
National Teaching Aids, Inc.

Parthenogenesis is a type of sexual reproduction in which an egg develops into a new individual without being fertilized by a sperm cell. Reproduction in some ants, BEES, and plant lice is parthenogenetic. Usually after several generations have been produced parthenogenetically, a biparental generation (stemming from two parents) occurs, and the eggs are fertilized. If parthenogenesis occurs among larval forms, the process is

Cross-section of a male hydra showing testes (T), where sperm is produced, and buds (B) which can break off to form separate animals.

Photomicrograph courtesy of
National Teaching Aids, Inc.

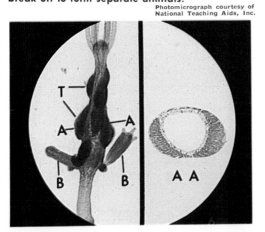

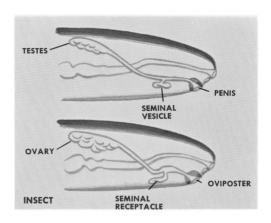

called *paedogenesis*. It is not a common method of reproduction. It is known to occur in one of the gallflies (*Miastor*). Immature forms produce eggs which develop into other larvae without fertilization.

About fifty years ago it was discovered that the eggs of some animals could be made to develop without fertilization. Various chemicals and mechanical stimulation took the place of fertilization. By these methods, sea urchins, frogs, and recently even a rabbit have been produced parthenogenetically.

Sexual reproduction usually takes place between adult animals, but in a few species mating by larval forms (*neoteny*) has been known to occur. *Axolotl,* the larva of the tiger salamander, mates and produces new larval forms which, under proper conditions, can become adult salamanders.

Metagenesis is the alternation of a sexual generation with an asexual one. Among COELENTERATA, alternation between the jellyfish (sexual) and the polyp (asexual) is an example of metagenesis.

In many plants and most animals the sexes are separate; the individuals are either male or female. Such plants or animals are *dioecious*. In *hermaphroditism,* both eggs and sperm are produced by the same individual. Since sexes are not separate in this type of reproduction, the plants or animals are called *monoecious*. Many of the lower invertebrates, such as the earthworm and the flatworms, are hermaphroditic. In most of these animals there is no self-fertilization, but rather different individuals come together (*copulate*) in order to exchange germ cells and ensure cross-fertilization.

Cross-fertilization is important because when germ cells from two individuals unite, each one gives to its new offspring a set of

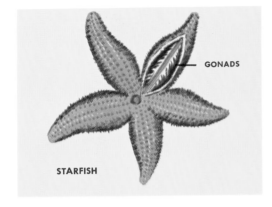

STARFISH

GONADS

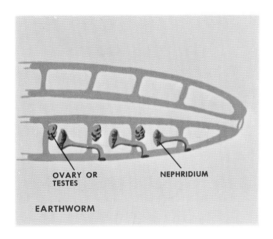

OVARY OR
TESTES

NEPHRIDIUM

EARTHWORM

Reproductive systems The most necessary part of a reproductive system is a *gonad*. The gonad may be an OVARY and produce eggs, or a TESTIS and produce sperm. Along with the gonads are other organs which help in the process of creating a new animal.

Some of these organs are sperm or egg-carrying tubes, organs for storing sperm, and glands for secreting liquids to help sperm to pass through ducts. There are glands secreting shells to protect eggs, and some that supply yolk to the egg. These feed the embryo, or young developing animal. In mammals (dogs, cats, humans), an organ called the *uterus* houses the developing embryo.

If animals have a permanent reproductive system, the number of parts and their structure vary, but the basic plan of the system remains the same.

A well-defined reproductive system with extra or accessory parts appears first among flatworms. PLANARIA are *monoecious,* that is each worm has both male and female organs. In the male system there are many small round testes along each side of the body. Each connects to a small tube, or duct (*vas efferens*). All the vas efferens on one side join a larger duct, the *vas deferens*. The two larger ducts enter a seminal vesicle which stores sperm until it is discharged through the penis. The muscular penis is used to transfer sperm to another flatworm, and opens into a tube (genital *atrium*) leading to the outside.

In the female system there are two ovaries, each opening into two tubes (oviducts). These join to form a larger tube, the vagina, connected to the genital atrium. Shells are added to the eggs in the atrium. Along the oviducts are yolk glands that add yolk cells to eggs passing down the oviducts. A seminal receptacle to receive sperm from another flatworm is connected to the vagina.

With minor variations, the same type of reproductive organs are found among ANNELIDA (earthworms) and ARTHROPODA

hereditary characteristics. Therefore, there is more variation among the members of the new generation. Those organisms that have inherited superior, or better, sets of characteristics fit best into their environment. They are more apt to survive and reproduce more of their kind.

Some monoecious animals and plants prevent self-fertilization by producing eggs and sperm (or pollen) at different times. In oysters the sperm are produced first (*protandry*.) The opposite condition where eggs are produced first is called *protogyny* and is rare.

An exchange of nuclear material between separate individuals takes place in primitive organisms such as the protozoan, *Paramecium,* and the alga, *Spirogyra*. There is no visible difference between the mating individuals, but a sexual reproductive process of *conjugation* shows that there are physiological differences.   J. C. K.

SEE ALSO: EMBRYOLOGY, REPRODUCTIVE SYSTEMS

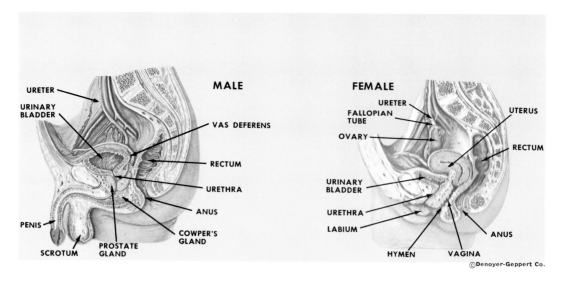

MALE — URETER, URINARY BLADDER, VAS DEFERENS, RECTUM, URETHRA, ANUS, PENIS, COWPER'S GLAND, SCROTUM, PROSTATE GLAND

FEMALE — URETER, FALLOPIAN TUBE, OVARY, UTERUS, RECTUM, URINARY BLADDER, URETHRA, LABIUM, ANUS, HYMEN, VAGINA

©Denoyer-Geppert Co.

(crayfish, insects, spiders). The crayfish and spider lack a penis to transfer sperm. Crayfish use their swimming legs to transfer sperm, while spiders use their second pair of legs (*pedipalpi*).

Since fertilization is external in starfish, accessory organs are lacking. The gonads connect to short ducts opening outside.

In man, testes develop in the body cavity and later descend into an external sac, the *scrotum*. In some mammals such as the rat, testes descend into the scrotum only during the breeding season. In the whale they remain permanently in the body cavity.

The human testes consist of many twisted tubules which connect to vas efferentia leading to part of the testes known as the *epididymis*. The coiled tube in the epididymis serves to store sperm and connects to the vas deferens. Where the vas deferens opens into the bladder duct (urethra), it is known as the *ejaculatory duct*. The urethra, an outlet for both sperm and urinary waste, opens outside through the penis. Three pairs of glands open into the vas deferens at different places. These secrete substances which lubricate the reproductive tubes and prevent sperm from being harmed by the acidity of the urine.

In the female, the human ovaries are located in the body cavity, closely associated with the expanded ends of the oviducts. The oviducts, called *Fallopian tubes* in the human, lead to a pear-shaped muscular organ, the uterus. It opens into a tube, the *vagina,* which serves as a birth canal.

During PREGNANCY, the uterus houses the developing embryo. While the egg is maturing in the ovary, the lining of the uterus is prepared for pregnancy. Hormones from the ovaries and pituitary gland cause it to thicken and its blood vessels to enlarge. If the mature egg is not fertilized after it breaks out of the ovary, a process called menstruation occurs. During MENSTRUATION the outer part of the uterine lining, parts of blood vessels, and glands are sloughed off and discarded.   J. C. K.

SEE ALSO: EMBRYOLOGY; MAMMALIA; REPRODUCTION, SEXUAL

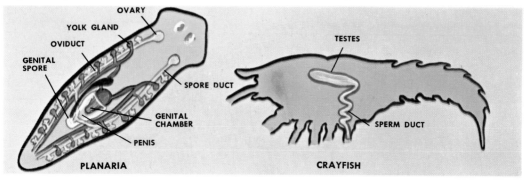

PLANARIA — OVARY, YOLK GLAND, OVIDUCT, GENITAL SPORE, SPORE DUCT, GENITAL CHAMBER, PENIS

CRAYFISH — TESTES, SPERM DUCT

Gopher tortoise of Southeastern U.S.

Reptilia (repp-TILL-ee-yuh) The name *reptile* is from a Latin word which means *to creep*. Reptiles are one kind of the animals with backbones (*vertebrates*). Many move by creeping or crawling. There are five groups of living reptiles: turtles, snakes, lizards, the New Zealand tuatara (*Sphenodon*) and the crocodilians, which include alligators and caymans. These present-day reptiles belong to the same group that once included dinosaurs, pterodactyls, and other prehistoric reptiles. All reptiles have scales on their skin, and most lay shelled eggs on land.

The first animals on Earth probably lived in the water. Reptiles were the first vertebrates to free themselves of water and live entirely on land. This change to land animals happened slowly, over millions of years. Even today, the *embryos* (baby animals before they are born or hatched) of reptiles, birds and mammals have fish-like gill openings. But these embryonic gills are never used for breathing, since baby reptiles also develop lungs. When they are born or hatched, they breathe air. Most reptiles now live on land, although some, such as crocodiles, alligators, and some turtles, still spend much of their lives in water.

Reptiles are covered with scales or horny plates which are formed from an outer layer of their skin (*epidermis*). They are cold-blooded animals; their bodies are the same temperature as the place where they happen to be. When out in the sun, their bodies are warm; when underground or in cool water, their bodies are cool. Because they are cold-blooded, reptiles live in warmer parts of the earth. Many kinds hibernate during the winter.

All reptiles except turtles have teeth, and all except snakes and a few lizards have two pairs of legs. Most reptiles lay eggs from which their babies hatch. The eggs of lizards and snakes have leathery skin. Those of turtles and CROCODILES are protected with strong shells. Some snakes and lizards are *ovoviviparous*—that is, the young are born live after hatching from their eggs within the mother's body.

In prehistoric times during the early MESOZOIC ERA, sometimes called the Age of Reptiles, reptiles were the most important group of animals on earth. They existed in huge numbers and in a wide variety of sizes and shapes. Dinosaurs, sea reptiles,

The American alligator has the horny hide typical of reptiles. Because they are cold-blooded, alligators live in warm climates.

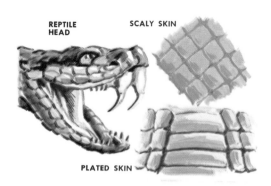

REPTILE HEAD

SCALY SKIN

PLATED SKIN

Some reptile characteristics: scaly skin, a jaw made of several bones, and the hatching of young from eggs

Buchsbaum

The sea turtle's legs are really flippers.

giant turtles, crocodiles, tuataras, and flying reptiles (pterosaurs) dominated the land for almost 140 million years. Toward the end of the Mesozoic Era, many of these reptiles became extinct. Those that survived became the ancestors of the presentday reptiles.

Class *Reptilia* includes more than 7,000 known species living today. The most abundant and thus best adapted group are the snakes and lizards. Scientists estimate that there are about the same number of species of these on earth as in past ages.

Biologists who study reptiles and amphibians are *herpetologists.*   D. J. A.

SEE ALSO: ALLIGATOR, CHORDATA, DINOSAUR, FOSSIL, LIZARD, SNAKE, TURTLE

Research Research takes place whenever a person uses careful methods of thinking and action in order to discover a truth. It may be a complicated *investigation* or *inquiry,* as when a trained scientist seeks a better explanation of puzzling natural events. Also, it may be a simpler study, such as one to find out which bite-size of cereal most people say they prefer.

In the days before modern science was developed, the main kinds of research were those related to literary or historical studies. Still another kind of research was, and still is, performed by the philosopher or theological student. In these types, they start from certain general principles and seek special evidence that they can logically show will fit the general principles. This is called *deductive* research.

During the seventeenth century, an Englishman, SIR FRANCIS BACON, wrote a treatise called *Novum Organum*. In this work Bacon set down the principles of *inductive* research (working from specific evidence to formulate general principles). This has come to be called the *scientific method* of research, and it has four major steps: observation, definition and hypothesis, experimentation, and verification.

Observations are made in laboratories and in nature of all the related sensory data connected with the problem that is being researched.

After originally limiting or *defining* the problem to be studied, the scientist makes field or laboratory observation or first trial *experiments*. Next, the scientist uses reasoning to create an "educated guess" or a trial statement *(hypothesis)* that explains what has been learned to date.

Next the scientist returns to the laboratory or field to derive general principles from observations and experiments. This step is called *verification*. In verification, any new observations must fit the hypothesis or else a new hypothesis must be devised.

Modern natural-science research is a combination of inductive-deductive reasoning, with an emphasis on inductive method. In research, every tool of discovery is used. Electronic devices and computers lend speed and accuracy to the results.

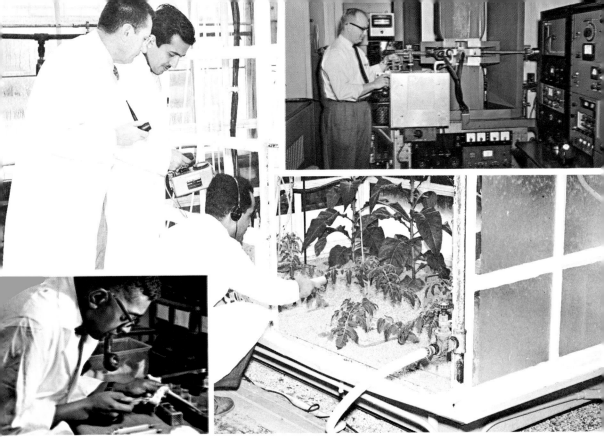

Daniel Oldfield; Argonne National Laboratory Photograph; American Oil Co.

(Left) Research scientist using white mice to determine causes of cancer; (center) Plant physiology research scientists conduct radioactive tracer experiments on tobacco and tomato plants; (right) Oil company scientist using mass spectrometer to determine composition of petroleum products

Unfortunately, many times no conclusions can be drawn, and the study is at least a partial failure. At other times it may be necessary to try different experiments and to seek new hypotheses.

Some research is done with no expectation of exactly where it may lead. Greater knowledge or possibly even more inquisitiveness are the motives in this type of research, which is known as *basic research.* Many now useful processes are based on the "useless" basic research of years ago.

In other cases research is directed toward the way knowledge may be applied to a particular problem. The search for a cure for cancer is *applied research.*

During the past 10 years the amount of knowledge has more than doubled. This doubling is due mainly to research. Most research occurs in university settings or in private industry. Research is funded mainly by the federal government or private industry.

Research is useful in almost every human concern. In agriculture it has improved crops and increased productiveness. Medical research has lengthened people's life span and made it more healthful. Market research brings people the material things they want. The social sciences, psychology, and educational research help people to learn.   D.A.B.

SEE ALSO: SCIENTIFIC METHOD

Reservoir (REZZ-er-vwahr) A reservoir is a natural or man-made lake where water supplies are stored.

Water stored in reservoirs is often used to provide cities with a water supply for everyday use. It may also be used to operate hydroelectric generators or to irrigate dry farmlands.

They have another very important use. In regions where heavy rainfall causes floods in river valleys, the great reservoirs store the excess water. They help prevent floods downstream from the DAM and provide deep water for navigation above the dam. Between rains this stored water may be released at a slow rate to supply the river below the dam with an even flow of water in dry weather.   V. V. N.

ANT
TRAPPED
IN RESIN

Amber is a fossilized resin

Resin (REZ-in) Resin is a substance that is obtained from the sap of trees that have cones. It is yellowish to dark brown in color. The sap flows from the tree through ducts, or it may be forced to flow by making an opening in the tree with a sharp knife.

There are synthetic resins which are chemically produced. These are important in the manufacture of PLASTICS and protective coatings. Synthetic resins are superior to natural resins in hardness and strength.

W. J. K.

Resistance (ree-ZISS-tuhns) In general, resistance is defined as an opposing force. In any work, when an object is moved, resistance must be overcome. The chief kinds of resistance act against electric current, gravity, friction, molecular masses, and change of mass motion (*inertia*).

Electrical resistance is the property of a material measured by the volts needed to pass a given current. This is stated in OHM'S LAW.

Gravity is the common type of resistance met every day. When lifting an object, a force greater than the pull of gravity must be exerted. This kind of resistance is easy to measure, either with a scale or balance.

A more difficult kind of resistance to measure is friction. Friction is caused when two objects rub against each other. The rougher the surface the greater the friction. This resistance occurs between the moving parts of machines.

The third kind of resistance, molecular forces, is divided into two categories, cohesion and adhesion. Cohesion is the attraction of like molecules, as observed in such materials as this piece of paper. Adhesion is the attraction of unlike molecules making it possible for the ink to stick to paper.

Inertia must be overcome to move or to stop any object. An object is said to have inertia of rest when it tends to stay at rest,

and inertia of motion when an object is in uniform motion and will continue to move in the same straight line unless acted on by an external force. Inertia is explained in Newton's first law of motion.   E. Y. K.

SEE ALSO: ADHESION; COHESION; FRICTION; GRAVITY; INERTIA; NEWTON, ISAAC; OHM

Resolution (rez-oh-LOO-shun) Resolution measures the ability to see detail. The greater the resolution, the better one can see the object studied.

The resolution of optical instruments depends on many factors. The resolution of a telescope depends greatly on an atmosphere free of clouds and pollutants. The microscope's resolution depends on the lens quality and the size of the *objective* or bottom lens.   A.J.H.

Resonance When an object is set into vibration with a certain pitch (*frequency*), any other nearby object that can vibrate at that same pitch will then start to do so. The vibrations of the second object are called *resonant,* or *sympathetic*, vibrations; and the two bodies are in *resonance* with each other.

To understand resonance, it must be remembered that it is harder to make a heavy object vibrate rapidly than it is a light one. A stiff spring tends to vibrate when plucked, more rapidly than does a heavy or "soggy" one. It is therefore *stiffness* (the amount of force needed to deform the object one unit distance) and *mass* (also called "heaviness") that determine the *resonant frequency,* or "frequency of easiest vibration," for a simple mechanical system. This may be expressed algebraically in the simple formula:

$$^{F}\text{vibrations/second} = 2\pi \sqrt{\frac{\text{Stiffness}}{\text{Mass}}}$$

The general principle holds that a heavy weight on a "soggy" spring will naturally vibrate slowly, whereas a light weight hung upon a stiff spring will naturally vibrate rapidly. Or a short, tightly stretched piano string will tend to vibrate faster than a loose, long one. In the electrical circuit, there are two basic properties associated with resonance. These are *capacitance* and *inductance*. Capacitance is a kind of "electrical elasticity" and is produced by devices called *capacitors*

1 Lift the covering lid of a piano while at the same time you press down on the right or sustaining pedal.

2 Hum or sing a loud, clear note into the open piano, with pedal held down.

3 Suddenly stop singing the note and listen. What note comes from the piano? Which string was in resonance with your voice?

(measured in *farads*). "Electrical heaviness" is associated with the property inductance, obtained by the use of wire coils or *inductors* (measured in *henrys*). One first chooses the proper-sized coil and capacitor by the formula:

$$\text{F vibrations/second} = 2\pi \sqrt{\dfrac{1}{(\text{henrys}) \times (\text{farads})}}$$

Then one makes the electrical circuit respond most favorably to a special alternating voltage that is to *resonate,* at that frequency, just as a string would respond to a sound wave striking it.   C. F. R.

SEE ALSO: ELECTRICITY, ELECTROMAGNETIC WAVE, MUSICAL INSTRUMENT

Resources see Natural resources

Respiratory system (rih-SPY-ruh-tohree) An animal uses its respiratory system to exchange carbon dioxide, a waste gas, for oxygen, a gas needed by its body. After the oxygen has been absorbed in the blood and food has been digested, the two act together to release the energy that is bound up in food and store it in a form that can be used by the body. As energy for body activities is produced, carbon dioxide is released. Muscular movement, digestion, and heart beat are examples of body activities that require energy.

There are four important kinds of respiratory systems found among animals. These are *moist skins* (in earthworms), *gills* (in fish) *tracheae* (in insects), and *lungs* (in many land animals). Both oxygen and carbon dioxide are usually dissolved in the blood and carried by the circulatory system. The blood, in contact with the moist walls of the skin, gills, or lungs, gives up its carbon dioxide and takes in oxygen.

RESPIRATION IN LOWER ANIMALS

In one-celled animals, respiration, or the exchange of waste carbon dioxide for oxygen, takes place through the cell wall. No respiratory system is needed. The cells of simple, many-celled animals, such as hydras, sponges, and many worms, also respire, or breathe, through their cell walls.

The annelid earthworm uses its moist skin for respiration. The skin is well supplied with blood vessels.

Cross-section of earthworm

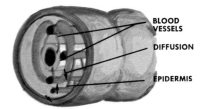

BLOOD VESSELS

DIFFUSION

EPIDERMIS

ARTHROPODS

Among arthropods there are several kinds of respiratory systems. Crayfish respire with gills. Their gills are fine, feather-like projec-

1453

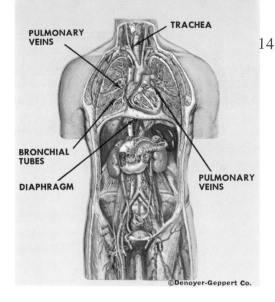

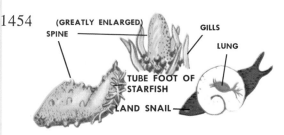

Human respiratory system

tions from the body wall. On each side of the thorax is a gill chamber in which there are two or three rows of gills. Blood is channeled from a large sinus (open space) to the gills where respiration takes place.

The insects, another group of arthropods, respire by means of finely-branched trachial tubes. These tubes go to all parts of the body. The largest tracheae connect to pairs of *spiracles* located along each side of the body. Contraction and expansion of the

Respiratory system of a grasshopper: (A) is a spiracle, or breathing hole

Photo-micrographs by National Teaching Aids, Inc.

abdomen has a pump-like action upon a group of air sacs. These force air in and out of the tracheal system through the spiracles. The finest branches, *tracheoles,* are connected directly to tissues where they deliver oxygen and remove carbon dioxide.

The spiders, also arthropods, have some tracheae, but most respiration is carried on through organs called *book lungs*. These are flat, thin, leaf-like air sacs.

MOLLUSKS

Among mollusks, respiration may take place through the mantle, by lungs or by gills. The mantle is a tissue layer covering the body organs and secreting the shell. The fresh water mussel breathes through the mantle and by means of a pair of gills

on either side of the foot. The common snail has a lung which is a modified part of the mantle well supplied with blood vessels.

ECHINODERMS

There are several interesting types of respiratory systems among echinoderms. Between the spines on the upper surface of a STARFISH are soft skin gills called *dermal branchiae*. These function in respiration. The body cavity (coelom) extending into the skin gills brings the body fluid close to the sea water for gas exchange. Free ameboid cells (amebocytes) circulate in the body fluid and also aid in respiration. Brittle stars, on the other hand, use their tube feet and *bursae* (sacs) for respiration.

The sea cucumber and sea urchin are other echinoderms. In the sea urchin gaseous exchange takes place through the walls of a ring of pouches around its mouth. Sea cucumbers breathe through two branched tubes called the *respiratory tree*. The tree, bathed by body fluid, is connected to a muscular cloaca (enlarged posterior or hind end of intestine). Contraction and expansion of the cloaca forces water in and out of the tree. Oxygen in the sea water is exchanged for carbon dioxide in the body fluid through the walls of the respiratory tree.

VERTEBRATES

The vertebrates breathe through gills, skin, or lungs, depending upon whether they live in water or on land. Most of the FISH respire through gills. Their gills are supported by bony arches and covered by a crescent-shaped operculum. The lung fishes in Africa breathe with a "lung" during dry seasons. The lung connects to the pharynx, and is actually a swim bladder.

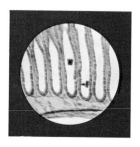

Gills of a fish. Water flows through at (W), and as it passes through sections of the gill at (F) the oxygen is taken into the blood

Photo-micrographs by National Teaching Aids, Inc.

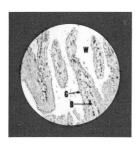

Outside gill of a salamander (G). Water flows past at (W), oxygen is taken in through skin, and carried by blood (B) throughout body

Photo-micrographs by National Teaching Aids, Inc.

The frog, an AMPHIBIAN, has gills in its aquatic tadpole stage. The adult frog, living on land, respires through its skin, mouth cavity, and lungs.

Reptiles, such as snakes and turtles, usually breathe through LUNGS. Birds breathe through lungs aided by a number of air sacs lying among the muscles and organs. These air sacs are connected to the bronchi (air tubes in the lungs). In birds the cavity surrounding the lungs is rigid, and the lungs do not expand like those of mammals. They are attached to ribs, and have a bellow-like action. Movements of the rib and abdominal muscles draw air into the lungs and air sacs. Contraction of the muscles in the thorax forces air out of the sacs and lungs. In flying, movement of the wing muscles forces air in and out of the sacs and lungs.

Man and other mammals breathe with lungs. They are covered by a thin epithelium, the pleura, and located in the chest cavity or thorax. The thorax and abdomen are separated by a flat, dome-shaped sheet of muscular tissue. This sheet of tissue is called the *diaphragm,* and its convex side faces the anterior, or head, region. When the ribs are raised and the diaphragm depressed, air enters and the lungs inflate. When the rib and diaphragm muscles relax, air is expelled and the lungs deflate.

The respiratory system in man consists of air passageways and lungs. Air enters the nostrils (*nares*) of the nose and goes into the nasal chamber. Air passes from the nasal chamber (lined with mucus-secreting epithelium) to the posterior nares connecting to the pharynx. From the pharynx, the air passes through the glottis, the opening to the larynx. The glottis is covered by a tissue flap called the *epiglottis.* Vocal cords are located in the larynx. The larynx connects to the largest air passageway to the lungs, the *trachea.* The trachea, a tube supported by a series of cartilage rings, divides into two *bronchi.* One bronchus goes to the right

CONSTRUCTING A RESPIRATORY MODEL

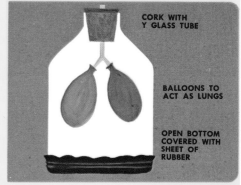

CORK WITH Y GLASS TUBE

BALLOONS TO ACT AS LUNGS

OPEN BOTTOM COVERED WITH SHEET OF RUBBER

1 Locate a large glass jar and remove the bottom. This may be done with a hot wire, glass cutter, or pouring in boiling water. Tape the cut edge to avoid injury while working with it.
2 A cork, with a hole drilled into it to insert a Y glass tube, is needed. On the ends of each fork place a balloon to serve as the lungs. A piece of inner tube or sheet rubber should be fastened over the bottom of the jar to mimic the diaphragm.
3 Push the diaphragm up into the jar with your clenched fist. The muscle is in this position (dome-shaped) when it is relaxed. What happened to the lungs (balloons)?
4 Release the pressure on the diaphragm. As the diaphragm in your body contracts, you take in air. When it relaxes, you expire air.

lung and another to the left. In the lung, the bronchus divides and redivides into smaller and smaller tubes. The smallest tubes are called *bronchioles,* and lead to the *air sacs* or *alveoli.* Walls of the alveoli are thin and moist, and gaseous exchange takes place through them.   L. M.

SEE ALSO: CIRCULATORY SYSTEM

Resurrection plant see Wild flowers

Resuscitation Resuscitation is the reviving of plants or animals which have apparently died. It commonly refers to the use of ARTIFICIAL RESPIRATION, cardiopulmonary resuscitation (CPR), or a pulmotor on people who have stopped breathing.

SEE ALSO: FIRST AID

Retch see Vomit

Reticulum see Ruminant

Retina see Eye

Retrograde motion The sun always moves through the sky in one direction. The motion of the planets is usually eastward. At times the motion of planets stops and loops westward. The change in motion of planets is retrograde motion.

Retrograde motion is caused by the different velocities of the planets. Earth has a greater velocity than Mars. As Earth catches up with Mars, the velocity of Mars seems to decrease. When Earth passes Mars, the path of Mars seems to reverse in the sky. Mars then loops back to its original direction.   A.J.H.

Retrorocket see Astronaut, Astronautics, Space travel, Space vehicles

Revolution A revolution is one complete turn around a given point. The term is used to describe the *orbit* of planets as they move around the sun as well as to give the speed of turning of certain types of engines. The speed of these engines is given as RPMS (revolutions per minute).

The time of one year is the time that it takes the Earth to revolve once around the sun. The Earth's oval path around the sun is called its orbit. The flat surface in which the orbit moves is the Earth's plane of orbit. The Earth revolves around the sun at the rate of about one degree per day and its year (period of revolution) is about 365 degrees. The path that a revolving body follows may be nearly circular or more like a flattened circle (*ellipse*).   H. S. G.
SEE ALSO: COPERNICUS, PLANETS, SOLAR SYSTEM, SPACE VEHICLES

Revolver see Weapons

Rh factor The Rh factor is found in the blood of 85 per cent of the population. People who have the factor in their blood are called *Rh-positive;* people who do not have it are called *Rh-negative*. The letters "Rh" are short for "Rhesus," the name of the kind of monkey used in research on this blood factor. Where transfusions (transfer of blood from one person to another) are needed, it is as important to know whether or not this factor exists in the blood as it is to know the blood type.

When blood from a person with the Rh factor (Rh-positive) is given by transfusion to another person with Rh-positive blood, there is no difficulty. If it is given to a person with Rh-negative blood, that person's blood will build antibodies against it. In small quantities, no great harm comes about, but repeated transfusions will increase the anti-Rh materials. The result is clumping, or *agglutinizing,* of the blood cells. This condition is so serious that further transfusions could result in death. To avoid this difficulty the blood is tested, or cross-matched, beforehand by mixing together blood from each person and examining it for clumping.

Another instance where difficulties arise is when an Rh-negative mother produces Rh-positive children (in such a case, the Rh factor is usually inherited by the children from an Rh-positive father). The mother's body may produce Rh antibodies if she has an unborn Rh-positive child. Though this condition is harmless with the first child, there may still be antibodies left in her blood during a second or third pregnancy. These antibodies can enter the blood of the unborn child and cause a reaction resulting in the destruction of the baby's red blood cells, to produce anemia and even death. Today, testing the mother's blood during pregnancy predicts possible difficulty and prepares the doctors to give compatible blood to the newborn baby.   D. J. I.
SEE ALSO: ANTIBODY, BLOOD, BLOOD TYPES, HEREDITY

Rhea see Birds, flightless

Rhenium (REE-ni-um) Rhenium is a rare metallic element used in electrical parts where rust resistance is needed. In nature, it is always found with other minerals. When prepared in its pure state, it is silver-white.

The element was isolated in 1925 by three German scientists, Berg, Noddack, and Tacke. In the United States, it occurs in traces usually with platinum and molybdenum ores in the southwest. Its best use is in electrical contact devices.

Rhenium (Re) has atomic number 75 and atomic weight 186.2. It occurs in 21 isotopes.   D.A.B.

SEE ALSO: ATOM, ELEMENTS

Rheostat A rheostat is a device which introduces a resistance into an electric circuit. The resistance can be varied and regulated, and the amount of the current changed. One use of a rheostat is to control theater lights.

Rhesus monkey see Rh factor

Rheumatic fever (roo-MAT-ick) This disease results from an allergic reaction of the body to a previous infection by the *streptococcus* bacteria, usually in the throat. It is occasionally caused by scarlet fever. The person with rheumatic fever (about 2% of patients with untreated "strep" throats) can develop stiff, red, swollen joints and a heart inflammation. The patient who does not stay in bed may suffer permanent heart damages.

Valves of the heart become scarred and the heart may enlarge to more than twice the normal size. The *mitral* valve is most often affected. The leaking valve will produce a heart murmur. Damaged valves can often be replaced in surgery by either plastic valves sewn in place or valves removed from a person who has recently died. Penicillin given at the time of the original "strep" infection seems to be the best way to prevent rheumatic fever.   B.M.H./E.S.S.

Rheumatism see Arthritis

Rhinoceros (rye-NAHSS-uh-russ) The word *rhinoceros* means "nose horn." Rhinoceroses have one or two horns which are made of hair cemented together. These animals are large, but not nearly so large as their

White rhino

James P. Rowan

prehistoric ancestor, Baluchitherium. It was 35 feet (10.7 meters) from nose to tail tip and 16 feet (4.9 meters) high at the shoulder.

Rhinoceroses (rhinos) are odd-toed Perissodactyla. Their legs are short and thick, and their three-toed feet rest on horny soles or platforms. There are five species of rhinos, three in Asia and two in Africa. All of them have very thick hides, scanty hair, massive heads, and small eyes. Vision is poor, but hearing is acute. They are vegetarians, grazing on grass. Molar and premolar teeth have broad grinding surfaces. Canine teeth are lacking, and the number of cutting teeth *(incisors)* varies with the species.

Rhinoceroses have one offspring at a time. Its weight is usually 100 pounds (45.4 kilograms). *Gestation* (the length of pregnancy) is 16 to 18 months. Young are slow in maturing, sometimes taking as long as five years to become adults. They may stay with their mothers for several years.

The great Indian rhinoceros has one horn, two lower incisors modified into tusks, and a heavy, armored skin. Those in Java are smaller, and females lack horns. The rhinoceros in Sumatra has two horns and a hairy coat. The African white rhinoceros is not white. The Afrikaans word *weit* means wide and refers to its wide lips, not to its color.   J.C.K.

Rhizoid see Moss

Rhizome (RYE-zohm) A rhizome is an underground STEM from which grow certain plants, such as iris and lily of the valley.

Although rhizomes grow underground as if they were roots, they have all the structures of stems, with nodes, internodes, buds and leaves. Buds and green, scale-like leaves develop at the nodes, the knotlike swellings on the rhizomes. Clusters of roots appear from the nodes on the underside of the rhizomes. Internodes are the spaces between the nodes.

Ferns and grasses have underground stems, and their leaves appear as their stems reach the surface. Cattails, sedges, and water lilies of marshes, as well as regular lilies, are spread by rhizomes.

Rhizomes reproduce by budding. Banana plants are started by cutting the rhizome into 3 to 4 pound (1.4 to 1.8 kilograms) pieces, each bearing at least one eye, or bud, and planting the pieces about a foot (.3 meter) deep in rows. A rhizome cut into pieces by a cultivating tool does not die, but each piece grows a separate plant.   P.G.B.

SEE ALSO: STEM, UNDERGROUND

Rhodium
Rhodium, atomic number 45, is a silver-white metallic element. It is one of the precious platinum metals. It was discovered in 1803.

Rhodium is extremely hard, with a melting point of 1,985° C. (3,605° F.). It occurs naturally with *platinum,* though in small quantities. Rhodium forms several reddish compounds.

Rhodium is used to plate other materials, giving a very bright, durable, and non-tarnishing surface. It is insoluble in nitric acid, sulfuric acid, and aqua regia, making it a more resistant material than gold and platinum. Rhodium-platinum alloys are used industrially where hot acids are involved and in thermocouples for high temperature measurement.

Rhodium (symbol Rh) has an atomic weight of 102.905.   D.J.I.

SEE ALSO: ATOM, ELEMENTS

Rhododendron
The rhododendron is one of the flowering shrubs. The blossoms, opening in the spring, range from pink through rose to purple. Rhododendron grows in the eastern part of the United States, particularly the southeastern states.

Rhododendron belongs to the genus *Azalea* and includes, among other flowering shrubs, the *azalea,* the *mountain laurel,* and *heather.* The rhododendron blooms in a cluster of predominantly white or rose-colored, bell-shaped flowers. Mountain laurel, an evergreen, blossoms earlier. The flower is a delicate pink cup about ½ inch (1.3 centimeters) across and grows in clusters of 20 or more blossoms. The rhododendron reaches a height of 3 to 20 feet (.9 to 6.1 meters).   M.R.L.

F. A. Blashfield

Rhododendron

Rhubarb
(ROO-bahrb) Rhubarb is an herb that grows year after year in cool climates. It has large leaves of which the greenish-pink petioles or leafstalks are eaten. The leaf blade and root have a poisonous material which can cause illness if eaten. But in some countries the dried root is used in medicine.

Rhubarb requires sandy soil. It is propagated by root and stem cuttings rather than seeds. A 5-foot (1.5-meter) flower stalk appears but should be removed since it takes away from the food supply needed for leaf formation. Rhubarb has more protein, vitamins, and minerals, and less carbohydrates, than many earth vegetables. The chief enemy is the fungus crown rot.   H.J.C.

Rib see Skeleton

Rib grass see Wild flowers

Riboflavin see Vitamin deficiency

Ribose see Nucleoprotein

Rice
Rice is a cereal grass native to Asia and Africa. It furnishes more than half of the people of the world with the main part of their food. Long-grained kinds of rice found in America have come from the Asiatic species.

A rice plant is an *annual* that grows 2 to 4 feet (.6 to 1.2 meters) tall. It has a round jointed stem, long pointed leaves, and seeds borne in dense heads on separate stalks. It needs more water than other grains in order to grow properly.

Rice is the main food of many peoples.

Rice Council: Harris Barnes, Jr.

Canadian wild rice or Indian rice, found growing around lakes in Canada and northwestern areas of the United States, is not related to the oriental rice and is not cultivated.   J. K. K.

SEE ALSO: CEREAL GRAINS

Richards, Dickenson Woodruff

(1895-1973) He was a U.S. physician who shared in the 1956 NOBEL PRIZE in physiology and medicine for his aids for studying heart diseases.

Dr. Richards helped develop *cardiac catheterization.* which involves passing a small tube along a vein and into the heart. This permits direct determination of the blood pressure and flow produced during heart contractions.   P.P.S.

Richardson, Sir Owen Willans

(1879-1959) In 1928 the NOBEL PRIZE for physics was given to Sir Owen Richardson, an English physicist. He developed the study of *thermionics,* which is the study of the emission of electrons or electricity from hot bodies.   A.J.H.

Richter Scale

The Richter Scale, a means for measuring energy released by an EARTHQUAKE at its source, was developed by C.F. Richter in 1935.

On the Richter Scale an earthquake of magnitude 3.0 has 10 times the energy of one at 2.0; one of 8.6 has three million times the energy of an earthquake of 5.0 magnitude. Earthquakes under 5 on the Richter scale are not serious, but over 5 the danger increases enormously.   P.P.S.

Rickets see Vitamin deficiency

Ridge

A ridge is a relatively narrow elevation that is characterized by its steep slopes. Most ridges occur where extensive rainfall erodes the slopes of small hills and mountains. The Blue Ridge Mountains of Virginia are a good example of a ridge system.

Rifle see Weapons

Rift valley

A rift valley is a landform that is produced by the splitting of a section of land bounded by two parallel rifts or faults. In the East African Rift Valley two sections of the earth's crust are ripping apart. This is caused by CONTINENTAL DRIFT.

Rigel see Orion, Stars

Ringworm

Ringworm is a disease of the skin caused by a *fungus,* a plant growth. It is not caused by a worm. Round patches of rough skin appear, often about the size of a nickel. The outer rim has many little bumps and may itch.   P.G.B.

SEE ALSO: FUNGUS, ATHLETE'S FOOT

Riptide see Tide

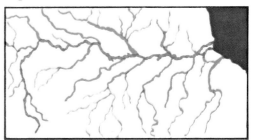

A river system is made of many smaller streams emptying into a main river.

River

A river is a stream of running water that carries to the sea much of the moisture that falls on the land. Different names are used to describe these streams, depending upon their size. River is the most common term for a large stream. Smaller streams are called *creeks,* while *brook* is the name for a very small stream.

Rivers are very important. They provide people with a means of transportation and a source of water. During floods they bring new soil to many areas.

A *river system* is made up of a main or large river and all of the smaller rivers and streams that feed into it. This system normally drains into the sea. The area that is drained by the river system is often referred to as a *drainage basin.* The area of the high-

James P. Rowan

In its upper course, a stream may be powerful enough to move rocks.

est land that lies between two drainage basins or river systems is called the *divide*.

Rivers are swiftest in the upper course, where the *gradient* of the stream is greatest (the slope of the bed is steepest). This is usually over 50 feet per mile (9 meters per kilometer). In the middle and lower courses, the gradient is much less, from 12 feet to a few inches per mile (2 meters to a few centimeters per kilometer).

The speed of a stream may be great enough in its upper course to move rocks and boulders. The power depends on the gradient, volume of water, and amount of material being carried—the more particles, the less velocity. As the stream levels out, gravel and silt drop. Islands and flood plains form, the latter being excellent crop-raising regions, at the expense of lands eroded in upper courses of the stream. In this way the Nile annually has given Egypt new fertility.

As the stream rushes along, uneven wearing of the bed may cause *cataracts* or *rapids*. Deep *canyons* or gorges may form, such as the Grand Canyons of the Yellowstone and Colorado Rivers which were formed in this way. Another spectacular sight is the waterfall formed when waters drop over the edge of a cliff. Sometimes the water finds softer materials under its bed above a falls and undermines the brink, leaving a scenic NATURAL BRIDGE.

Where great deposits of silt can drop undisturbed into the sea, a great *alluvial plain* forms. In cases where the mouth (end of the river) broadens and the tides can run upstream, large estuaries or inlets are developed. These make good ports.

Rivers are important to people. Rivers make rich flood plains for agriculture. They provide transportation for ships and power for mills. Early colonial America developed upstream from the sea at sites where mills could be built. After that, civilization paused, until people discovered and developed other sources of power or felt the desire to penetrate the continent. So important are rivers that major cities all over the world are located in advantageous positions along them. D.J.I.

SEE ALSO: DAM, EROSION, FLOOD, WATERFALL, WATERSHED

Roasting metal see Metal

Robbins, Frederick Chapman (1916-　) He is a U.S. *pediatrician* who shared in the 1954 NOBEL PRIZE for physiology and medicine with J.F. Enders and T.H. Weller for their *polio* research.

Dr. Robbins' first researched contagious diseases. In 1948, he joined Enders and Weller to work on cultivating viruses in tissue cultures. Because of bacteria contamination, viruses had been grown only in living tissue. However, by employing antibiotics to the supply of blood that kept the tissue alive, the doctors overcame this problem. The techniques they developed for cultivating the poliomyelitis virus in tissue culture made possible the development of polio vaccine. P.P.S.

Robin Robins are garden birds belonging in the thrush family. They have brown backs and red breasts. Young show their kinship with the thrush by developing spotted breasts after the first molt. They eat worms, insects, and berries.

Robins fly south for the winter and return in the spring, sometimes quite early. They migrate at the rate of about 38 miles (61 kilometers) a day. Soon after their return, they breed. They have only one mate in a season but may raise two to three broods. During courtship they display their bright red breasts. Nest building takes 6 to 20 days. The length of time for this depends upon the weather; rainy days slow down their building activity. They usually build their mud and grass nests in trees or sometimes on the ground.

Females lay from four to six bluish-green eggs and incubate them 12 to 14 days. Young remain nestlings for another 10 to 14 days. After leaving the nest, they are fledglings for another week or two. J.C.K.

Robinson, Sir Robert (1886-1975) He was a British organic chemist who was awarded the 1947 NOBEL PRIZE for his work on *alkaloids* and other vegetable products. His work aided in the development of various drugs.

Robinson first researched pigments that produced color in various flowers and particular kinds of wood. His later work included the alkaloids by first defining the arrangement of atoms in *morphine* and other alkaloids found in the seed of poppies. By establishing this basis, he was able to synthesize alkaloids, plant pigments, and other natural products from plants.   P.P.S.

Robot A robot is a computer-controlled mechanical arm, hand, or manipulator. Robots move parts, tools, or devices through a series of motions. To change the motions, one alters the programmed computer instructions that guide the robots.

Robots are at the forefront of factory automation, in some cases performing tasks too boring or too dangerous for humans. Industrial robots were invented in the United States, with most patents issued around 1954. An American company, Unimation, unveiled the first model in 1960. But since then, use and mastery of robots has become a Japanese specialty. As of 1982, Japan had 32,000 operating industrial robots. By contrast, the United States had only 7,000 and Western Europe 9,000.

Today researchers are working in an advanced computer specialty field called *artificial intelligence,* whose goal is to enable robots to see and feel through use of computer-controlled sensory devices. This second generation of robots is already emerging. In fact, in one plant in Japan, robots are helping to make other robots.

Rocket The term *rocket* applies to a type of vehicle propelled by a rocket engine. These engines may be liquid- or solid-fueled. They do not depend upon the atmosphere to operate. For this reason, the rocket is the basic source of power for travel in the near-vacuum of the space environment.

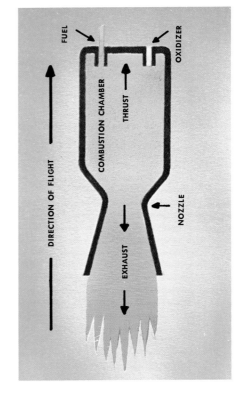

This diagram of a rocket engine shows the type of engine used in the Apollo missions.

Small rockets are popular in their use for fireworks displays, dating back to the Chinese invention of "fire arrows" about A.D. 1220. Rockets were reported to have been used by the Chinese in battle against attacking Mongols in A.D. 1232. They have since been used in many wars. During the War of 1812, bursting rockets inspired the writing of the "Star Spangled Banner."

Rockets today vary greatly in size and uses. Small rockets with explosive warheads are fired from hand-held launchers on the battlefield. Others are launched from attacking aircraft. Large rockets called *intercontinental ballistic missiles* (ICBM) with atomic warheads are awesome weapons. Other huge rockets serve as *launch* vehicles to place satellites and other payloads into space.

An American scientist, Dr. Robert H. Goddard, Professor Herman Oberth of Germany, and the USSR's Konstontin E. Tsiolkovsky share the honors of laying the foundation of modern rocketry through their pioneering work during the 1920s. Dr. Goddard continued to become recognized as the world's foremost rocket scientist prior to World War II.

Rockets may be classified in several ways. However, almost all have a streamlined cylindrical airframe with the payload attached at one end along with the guidance and control systems. The largest part of the rocket body is taken up with the chemical propellant tanks. The engine and exhaust nozzles are located at the bottom of the airframe.

The rocket engine is a reaction engine based upon Sir Isaac Newton's three laws of physical motion. These laws are: (1) a body remains at rest or in a state of motion in a straight line unless acted upon by an external force; (2) a force acting upon a body causes it to accelerate in the direction of the force, the acceleration being directly proportional to the force and inversely proportional to the mass of the body; and, (3) to every action, there is an equal and opposite reaction.

When the fuel and oxidant are burned in the rocket engine's combustion chambers, a vast amount of expanding gas is generated, creating enormous pressures. As the gases rush out of the open engine nozzle, a reaction or equal force is created in the opposite direction. This force, called *thrust,* acts against the forward wall of the combustion chamber and causes the rocket to move. As long as the propellants are expelled as hot gases, they will produce a continuous thrusting force. The amount of thrust generated is measured in pounds or kilonewtons, and is determined by two major factors: *rate* at which the propellants are burned, and *velocity* at which the resulting gases are exhausted through the nozzle. Simply stated, *thrust equals propellant flow rate × exhaust velocity.*

Propellant efficency is measured by its *specific impulse* (amount of thrust from each pound or kilogram of propellant for one second of engine operation). It compares to the miles per gallon or kilometers per liter of automobile fuel performance. The refined kerosene-liquid oxygen propellants have a specific impulse of 300 seconds, while the newer liquid hydrogen-liquid oxygen propellants reach about 400 seconds.

Obviously a rocket must have a favorable thrust-to-weight RATIO for a successful flight mission. For lift-off, the initial thrust must sufficiently exceed the total weight of the vehicle. For example a 5:4 ratio at launch will permit lift-off and initial acceleration. As the rocket gains altitude, the weight decreases as the propellants are consumed and the distance from the Earth is increased. Thrust also increases as the atmospheric pressure drops. As a consequence, acceleration continues to increase until the propellant is exhausted or the flow is shut off by closing the fuel-system valves.

Staging or sectioning the rocket vehicle is often used to achieve a more favorable *mass* ratio. When the propellant is exhausted in the first or lower stage of the rocket, the airframe section with its engine and propellant tanks is detached and discarded. A second rocket engine is then ignited and accelerates the lightened rocket to higher speeds. Several stages may be used.

Solid-fuel rockets have the combined fuel and oxidizer in a thick liquid form poured into the body cavity of the airframe. It then hardens into a solid material resembling rubber. A core is then removed to allow for a burning chamber. The shape of the core determines to a large extent the thrust characteristics of the engine. The solid-propellant rocket engine has the advantage of being storable and ready for instant firing.

Small rockets are usually solid-fuel types. Most of the larger rockets have so far used a liquid propellant. The combustion can be easily controlled with the simple closing or opening of a valve. Also, the liquid propellants yield a higher specific impulse. The liquid-fuel rocket has the fuel and oxidizer stored in separate tanks. High pressure turbo pumps force the two liquids into the engine combustion chamber where ignition takes place. A variety of fuel-oxidizer combinations can be used, depending upon the engine design and the mission requirements.

The *Titan III* launch vehicle is an interesting example of combining a basic liquid-propellant rocket with two strap-on, solid-fuel rockets to increase the lift-off capability.

Future rocket-propulsion systems will undoubtedly include nuclear engines along with a variety of other types for use while in space. Among these are gas-heating, electric propul-

NASA

The specific impulse of a rocket measures the amount of thrust it produces per second of operation.

sion, and ion engines, and photon-propulsion systems.

Rockets depend upon sensitive guidance and control systems for their flight mission success. Several types of these are used including the *inertial, semi-inertial, radio* (or *command*), *celestial* (or *star tracking*), and *infrared*. Inertial guidance systems are self-contained and independent of outside influences. They utilize accelerometers, memory devices such as on-board computers, and gyroscopes. Once programmed, this guidance system can direct the rocket to any destination either back on earth or in space. The rocket engines are *gimbeled* so that directional control commands can be carried out. The semi-inertial system has additional equipment on board, enabling it to receive new program instructions for course modification. The infrared system relies upon the heat given off by objects. This heat is detected by a photoelectric device. The variations are translated into guidance information, and they control the rocket's course. The so-called heat-seeking missiles are military weapons.

The largest United States rocket so far was *Saturn V*, designed for the NASA Apollo missions. It was 365 feet (111 meters) high with its payload attached. The first stage was 33 feet (10 meters) in diameter and contained five rocket engines, which developed about 7,500,000 pounds (33,340 kilonewtons) of thrust at lift-off.   R.J.J.

SEE ALSO: MISSILE, ROCKET ENGINE, ROCKET PROPELLANT, SPACE STATION, SPACE TRAVEL, SPACE VEHICLES

Rocket engine A rocket engine is an engine that can provide a great amount of power. There are several types of rocket engines. Each one uses difference sources of energy. The chemical rocket is the most common today; however, more advanced types are being developed.

The rocket engine is a *reaction* engine. Its principle relates to Newton's laws of physical motion, especially the third law which states that for every action there is an equal and opposite reaction. In the chemical rocket, the propellant is burned in the engine combustion chamber. As the rapidly expanding gases exhaust through the engine nozzle, a *thrust* is created and moves the vehicle forward.

The performance limitations of chemical rockets make it necessary to develop new propulsion systems with greater performance characteristics. Long-term space missions over extreme distances are not within the practical capabilities of power now available with the chemical rockets. Several systems are now being researched.

The rocket engine is part of an overall *propulsion system* which generally has five components: a source of energy, a propellant system, a fuel-flow system, a thrust unit, and a cooling system.

All propulsion systems are basically *energy-storage* and *energy-conversion* systems. The generation of thrust in the engine is often only the final step in a series of steps of energy conversions. The generation of thrust in the engine is characterized by conversion of energy from some previous form to kinetic energy (exhaust velocity) of the discharged particles (propellant or expellant) according to the opposite-reaction principle. Thus propulsion systems are best classified according to the energy form by which the thrust proper is generated, instead of by the form of energy which produced the beginning thrust.

This classification yields four basic

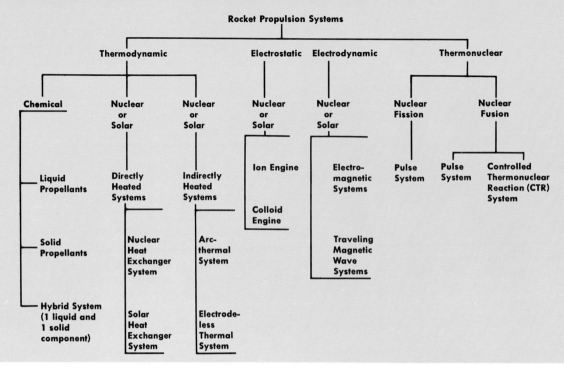

families of rocket propulsion systems: (1) thermodynamic systems, (2) electrostatic systems, (3) electrodynamic systems, (4) thermonuclear systems. The systems belonging to each family are surveyed above. Essentially, in the *thermodynamic* system, a hot gas is produced and then expanded in the exhaust nozzle. This hot gas can be produced by COMBUSTION (chemical systems); by heating a gas (for instance, hydrogen); by means of heat from a nuclear reactor or focused solar radiation *(directly heated systems);* or by means of an electric arc or other methods (called *indirectly heated* systems, because the energy, instead of being transferred directly to the gas in the form of heat, is first converted to electric energy that fires an electric arc which, in turn, heats the propellant gas).

Of the two primary energy sources, the nuclear is more versatile than the solar because the solar is less concentrated and becomes altogether too weak at distances beyond the planet Mars. In the *electrostatic* system the propellant material is transformed into electrically-charted particles which are accelerated in an electrostatic field toward the electrode of the opposite charge, that is, positively-charged particles are accelerated toward the CATHODE (negative electrode) and negatively-charged particles are accelerated toward the ANODE (positive electrode). By piercing the respective electrode, the particles are discharged

at great speed. If these particles are charged atoms, they are called *"ions";* if they are larger than atoms (molecules), they are called *"colloids."* Positive ions, which are atoms deprived of one electron each, are more easily produced than negative ions. Successful experiments have been conducted with ion engines using positive cesium ions or mercury ions. In the *electrodynamic* systems ("plasma systems"), such a hot gas is produced (10,000 to 40,000° F. or 5,500 to 22,200° C.) that it is no longer neutral like a normal hot gas, but partly decomposed into positive ions and negative electrons. This gas (called a PLASMA) conducts electric current, and can therefore be accelerated by suitably applied electric and magnetic fields. The theory of the very complex motion of a plasma gas under the influence of electric and/or magnetic fields belongs to the science of magneto-fluid-mechanics. A typical propellant for electrodynamic systems is hydrogen.

Finally, the *thermonuclear* systems can be loosely divided into *nuclear fission pulse* systems (propulsion by means of small atomic bombs exploding successively in the back of the spaceship) and into *nuclear fusion* systems. Here the CTR (controlled thermonuclear reaction) system is of particular significance. It represents, in the field of nuclear reactions, the counterpart of the combustion rocket in the field of chemical reactions. Instead of burning carbon and

Rocket engine

oxygen to CO_2, or hydrogen and oxygen to H_2O, the CTR-system "burns" helium, the nucleus of which contains two protons and one neutron (^3He); and deuterium (heavy hydrogen) to helium, the nucleus of which contains two protons and two neutrons (^4He). The gas temperature, 4,000 to 7,000° F. (2,200 to 3,870° C.) in chemical rockets, is about 100 million degrees F. (or about 55 million degrees C.) in a CTR-system, because the energy output per unit exhaust mass is about one million times greater in the CTR-system than in the chemical system. In spite of the many technical problems associated with the CTR-system, there is reason to believe that it can be in practical operation within the next twenty to thirty years.

Liquid and solid chemical agents are currently used in missiles and in spacecraft such as the Space Shuttle. Scientists also are working on the development of nuclear and electric rockets for space travel. Because of their importance, these four propulsion systems are discussed in more detail.

LIQUID PROPELLANT ENGINE

The principal parts of a liquid system are the propellant tanks, the propellant feed system, the injector, the combusion chamber, and the expansion nozzle. Nozzle and chamber are cooled by the fuel which is ducted through a cooling jacket before passing through the injector into the combusion chamber. A propellant feed system, either a turbopump or high-pressure gas, forces the propellants from the tanks into the injector.

In large rocket vehicles, this pressure can be applied within acceptable structural weight limits only by turbopump systems. In space, chemical rocket engines can also be applied effectively at low chamber pressures. In low pressure systems the thrust unit is comparatively large and heavy. The injector distributes the oxidizer and fuel into a flow pattern which causes thorough mixing when the fluids enter the combustion chamber. Since the feed system, at the same time, is a metering system, controlling the quantity of oxidizer and fuel, the total massflow per second into the combustion chamber is either constant or varies according to a preset program; and, furthermore, the ratio of oxidizer to fuel *(mixture ratio)* is constant. Ignition occurs almost immediately after the fluids have been injected, that is, near the face of the injec-

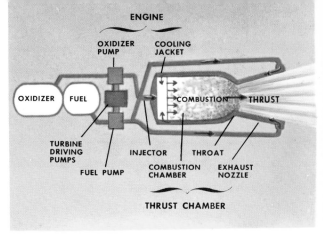

Chemical liquid rocket engine

tor. Initial ignition is provided by a spark plug or a chemical ignition device; thereafter, the heat of the combusion gas assures continued ignition. The combustion process is rapid. Most of it is completed in the combustion chamber. In a well-designed thrust chamber very little combustion occurs in the throat or in the nozzle.

The combustion process consists of the following steps: collision of the injected fluid, atomization and mixing, vaporization, and chemical reaction. The thermal energy (heat) released through combustion raises the gas to a high temperature and pressure, and thereby produces the beginning conditions required for the acceleration of the gas mass relative to the rocket, hence, the generation of thrust. The acceleration occurs in the so-called *de Laval nozzle* (named after its inventor), and consists of two steps: acceleration in a *convergent* section which reaches its smallest diameter in the throat where the gas speed has attained local sound velocity; and further acceleration in the *divergent* portion (exhaust nozzle) which is required to speed the gas to supersonic velocity, once sonic speed is reached.

SOLID PROPELLANT ENGINE

Generally, the solid propellant system is simpler, while the liquid propellant system has the advantage of versatility and high performance. The solid system actually consists only of the engine proper, if one is to be consistent with the definitions applied to the liquid system. Principal engine components are the propellant, the chamber, the igniter, and the nozzle. The entire body of a solid propellant is referred to as the *grain*.

The grain contains both oxidizer and fuel. After ignition, all exposed surfaces burn in such a way that the propellant is consumed in a direction normal to the burning surface (such as from the center outward to the

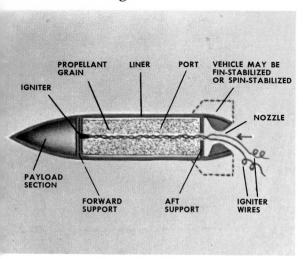

Chemical solid rocket engine

chamber wall). The grain material, size, and geometrical form, and the shape of the burning surface (cross-section of the port is circular or star-shaped, for example) determine chamber pressure, thrust, and duration of burning. Close control of burning characteristics and propellant design is required to avoid damage to the uncooled nozzle and chamber wall. To reduce the danger of damage, the chamber wall is sometimes protected by a liner of heat-resisting material.

Almost all igniters are of the pyrotechnic type. They consist of a temperature-sensitive primer which can be set off by an electric current and which, in turn, ignites the igniter powder charge. Hot gases from the powder charge stream down the port and quickly ignite all of the exposed grain surface all the way down to the aft support. Since the nozzle is not cooled, one of two principal design approaches can be used: the *thermal capacitance nozzle* is used for very short duration firings and the *insulated nozzle* for longer durations. The latter uses heat resistant liners, such as ceramics or graphite.

Despite its lower performance (higher propellant consumption per amount of thrust generated per second) than liquid systems, solid rockets are used today as space booster propulsion systems. The solids are competitive with the liquids in this field, (1) because boosters (first stages of rocket vehicles) usually do not necessarily require the versatility offered by liquid systems at the price of greater complexity, (2) because high performance is

needed less in the booster stage than in upper stages, (3) because the simplicity of solids allows large units of several million pounds or kilonewtons of thrust to be used as boosters for space shuttles. Two such solid rocket boosters (SRBs) are used to launch shuttles into orbit, and are parachuted back to earth for reuse.

NUCLEAR ENGINE

In the nuclear heat-exchanger system chemical reaction as the source of energy is replaced by controlled nuclear fission, that is by the decay of uranium atoms into atoms of lighter elements. This decay, or fission, is triggered and sustained by neutrons which are released as a result of the fission process. The intensity of the fission process can be speeded up or slowed down by means of rods of strongly neutron-absorbing materials (for example, cadmium) which can be pushed into the reactor. The cadmium rods keep the rate of nuclear fission at a moderate level, thereby preventing the reactor from turning into an actual atom bomb. The rods are called *moderators*.

Fission can be visualized as *explosion* of the very complex uranium (U^{235}) atoms. Fission is intensified radioactively, the intensification being caused by higher purity of the radioactive material and higher concentration of neutrons trapped within the reactor shell which contains neutron reflecting material. The fragments of the exploding uranium atoms are slowed down in the reactor, and thereby heat the reactor material. The primary energy produced by the reactor is, therefore, thermal, as in the case of chemical reaction, but caused by a different process. (The control rods absorb energy to prevent overproduction of heat that would otherwise melt the reactor itself or overload the cooling fluid—coolant.) The base material contains the uranium mixed with it, and makes up the structural frame of the reactor. Pure uranium would not be suitable because (1) it is too heavily concentrated as an energy source for a reactor, (2) it is not heat resistant enough, (3) it is too expensive to obtain.

Suitable base materials are, in the order of increasing heat sensitivity, graphite, tungsten, and nitrates of some rare earths (such as niobium nitrate). Most work is now done with graphite reactors which might be the first ones used in a nuclear rocket engine. Use of graphite restricts the

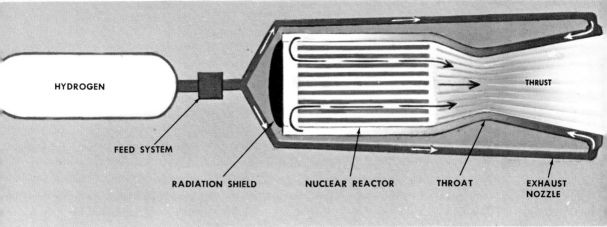

Nuclear heat exchanger propulsion system and its principal parts

HYDROGEN

FEED SYSTEM

RADIATION SHIELD

NUCLEAR REACTOR

THROAT

THRUST

EXHAUST NOZZLE

operational temperature range of reactors to 3,500 to 4,000° F. (1,930 to 2,200° C.) corresponding to the lower regions of combustion temperatures. This does not prevent a reactor from producing much more energy than a chemical rocket, because fluids can be used in nuclear engines which are capable of absorbing much more energy at the same temperature (that is, have higher heat capacities) than the fluids available in chemical rockets. The latter ones are mostly combustion products, primarily carbon dioxide (CO_2) and water (H_2O).

No oxidizer is needed, of course, in a nuclear engine. A single fluid is sufficient. On the basis of highest heat capacity per pound, as well as several other characteristics, hydrogen is the most efficient propellant for nuclear engines. As a result, the graphite reactor pumps about four times as much energy into each pound of propellant (hydrogen) than does a chemical rocket, in spite of the lower temperatures involved. The hydrogen absorbs this energy by flowing through the many ducts in the reactor which expose the greatest graphite-uranium surface to the hydrogen.

In a nuclear engine the propellant gas is, therefore, heated by serving as coolant for the reactor. When starting a nuclear heat exchanger engine, the control rods are pulled out enough to heat the reactor structure to a fraction of its operational temperature to avoid excessive heat stresses on the graphite structure. Then hydrogen flow sets in. After a few seconds, heat production and hydrogen flow are gradually increased until operational conditions are reached. When terminating thrust generation, the propellant cannot simply be shut off as in a chemical engine, since this would cause the reactor to melt. The first step is to lower the control rods, thereby shutting off neutron production. It takes a while

(minutes), however, until the existing fission process has fallen to a level at which it can no longer damage the uncooled reactor. The hydrogen flow must be maintained during this time, though at a gradually diminishing rate. When the hydrogen flow is finally shut off, fission is by no means zero. Even after a week the radiation is still too strong for humans to approach the reactor unprotected.

ELECTRIC ENGINES

Electric propulsion systems use electric power to produce thrust. Rocket engines of this type can operate much longer than other rocket engines but produce less thrust.

There are three main types of electric engines: arc jet engines, plasma jet engines, and ion engines. *Arc jet engines* heat a propellant gas with an electric spark called an *electric arc*. This method heats the propellant to a temperature three or four times greater than that produced by a solid- or liquid-propellant rocket. *Plasma jet engines* are similar to arc jet engines. An electric arc is used to heat the propellant gas. However, the gas contains some electrically charged particles. The mixture of gas and particles is called *plasma*. Because the plasma has a net charge, electric fields and magnetic fields can be used to increase the speed at which the plasma flows through the rocket. *Ion engines* contain heating coils that change the fuel into vapor. This vapor then flows over a special grid, called an *ionization grid*, and is changed into electrically charged particles called *ions*. The ions are accelerated to tremendous speeds using an electric field. Early versions of the ion-drive engine were first flown in orbit in 1969.   K.A.E./D.D./M.K.H.

SEE ALSO: ASTRONAUTICS, FUEL, HYDROGEN, MISSILE, NUCLEAR ENERGY, NUCLEAR REACTORS, ROCKET, ROCKET PROPELLANT, SPACE VEHICLES

Rocket propellant Rocket propellants are fluids which are accelerated in the rocket engine and driven out at high speed, thereby producing the sudden push, or thrust, which pushes forward, or propels, the rocket vehicle. Different propellants are used in the various rocket propulsion systems described in ROCKET ENGINES. Only in the chemical and in the thermonuclear systems does the propellant serve as the major source of energy, as well as a means producing thrust. In all other cases, (that is, in the nuclear, thermodynamic, electrostatic, and electrodynamic systems) the propellant is merely a thrust generator, while the primary energy source is separate and is in the form of a nuclear reactor or concentrated solar radiation.

Liquid propellants for chemical systems consist of the *oxidizer* and the *fuel*. Usually these fluids are separate (*bipropellant*), but in some liquids they are combined (*monopropellant*). A monopropellant can either be a mixture (for example, hydrogen peroxide and alcohol) or a chemical compound (as examples, hydrogen peroxide or nitromethane).

Monopropellants are simpler in design, since they require only one propellant tank and one pump. These advantages are offset usually by sensitivity to shock and heat which makes them explode easily in everyday handling. They generally perform more poorly than the bipropellants. So far only two monopropellants have attained practical significance, hydrogen peroxide and hydrazine, both for use only in auxiliary engines (such as control engines) because of inferior performance.

In the bipropellants, the oxidizer is rated on its chemical "aggressiveness." What makes the atom of an oxidizer chemically reactive (that is, ready to enter a reaction) is a quality called "electronegativity," a lack of just one electron to fill up the outermost of the atom's electron shells. Fuels consist of elements which have their respective atomic electron shells filled up and possess the first electron to fill the next shell. In a chemical reaction, oxidizer and fuel com-

TABLE I—CHARACTERISTIC PERFORMANCE DATA OF LIQUID PROPELLANT COMBINATIONS

OXIDIZER	FUEL	OXIDIZER-TO-FUEL RATIO	COMBUSTION TEMPERATURE F.°	COMBUSTION TEMPERATURE C.°	THRUST Pounds per second	THRUST Kilonewtons per second
	RP-1	2:1	5570°	3080°	270 (310)*	1.20 (1.38)*
	Hydrazine, N_2H_4	.7:1	5370°	2970°	280 (320)	1.24 (1.42)
	Hydrogen, H_2	8:1	5870°	3240°	325 (380)	1.44 (1.69)
Liquid	Hydrogen, H_2	3.5:1	4500°	2480°	370 (425)	1.64 (1.89)
Oxygen, O_2	JP-4	2.6:1	7100°	3930°	280 (315)	1.24 (1.40)
	Hydrazine, N_2H_4	2:1	7740°	4280°	315 (355)	1.40 (1.58)
	Hydrogen, H_2	19:1	8530°	4720°	335 (390)	1.49 (1.73)
	Hydrogen, H_2	4.5:1	5000°	2760°	375 (435)	1.67 (1.93)
Red Fuming Nitric Acid (RENA) HNO_3—22% NO_2	JP-4	4.1:1	5150°	2840°	230 (265)	1.02 (1.18)

* The numbers in parentheses indicate the thrust attainable in space as opposed to that attainable on earth's surface.

TABLE II—PERFORMANCE DATA OF THE FOUR PRINCIPAL FAMILIES OF ROCKET PROPULSION SYSTEMS

PROPULSION SYSTEM	THRUST Pounds per seconds	Kilonewtons per second	TEMPERATURES F.°	C.°
Thermodynamic				
Solid propellants	200-230	.89-1.02	5,000-7,000°	2,760-3,870°
Liquid propellants	300-450	1.33-2.00	4,000-8,000°	2,200-4,430°
Solar heat exchanger	500-600	2.22-2.67	about 3,500°	about 1,930°
Nuclear heat exchanger	700-850	3.11-3.78	about 4,000°	about 2,200°
Arc-thermal	1,000-1,500	4.45-6.67	6,000-10,000°	3,320-5,540°
Electrostatic				
Ion system	3,000-30,000	13.34-133.45		
	(Cesium or mercury)			
Colloid systems	2,000-3,000	8.90-13.34		
Electromagnetic				
Electrodynamic	4,000-20,000	17.79-88.96	10,000°+	5,000°+
Traveling magnetic wave	1,000-3,000	4.45-13.34	10,000°+	5,000°+
Thermonuclear				
Fission, pulsed	3,000-4,000	13.34-17.79	1,000,000°+	555,000°+
Fusion, pulsed	5,000-10,000	22.24-44.48	100 million°+	55 million°+
Controlled Thermonuclear				
Reaction System	20,000-200,000	88.96-889.64	100 million°+	55 million°+

bine to share the "excess electron" of the fuel atom. Fluorine has the highest electronegativity of all oxidizers, and is therefore most reactive, causing the greatest heat release. Certain properties have limited its use.

Presently the principal oxidizer is liquid oxygen. A fuel is rated on its energy release per unit weight. The most favorable fuel is liquid hydrogen which yields the highest energy release and has other favorable qualities. Its principal disadvantage is low density, which so far has limited its use to upper stages of space boosters. The most common fuel of large rockets today is RP-1, a jet fuel containing carbon and hydrogen. The principal characteristics of some important liquid propellants are listed in Table I.

The most important performance characteristic of any propellant is the specific impulse (Isp), defined as the pounds per sec. High Isp is desirable, because that means that the rocket gets more thrust out of a certain amount of propellant.

Solid propellants can be divided into two principal groups, (1) the *composite* propellant, consisting of an inorganic oxidizer broken up and scattered in organic plastic (fuel); (2) the *double-base* propellant, con-

sisting of the colloid of nitroglycerin-nitrocellulose. Some common oxidizer crystals used in composite propellants are from the perchlorate and inorganic nitrate families. They are dispersed in fuels which have a base of asphalt-oil, plastic, or rubber. Some of the common double-base propellants are from the organic nitrate family. Solid propellants show a lower specific impulse than most liquids, around 220-230 lb. (980-1,020 newtons) thrust.

A survey of the specific impulse range of all four major families of rocket propulsion systems is presented in Table II. It is seen that the solar heat exchanger system, the arc-thermal system, the family of electrostatic systems and of electromagnetic systems, as well as the controlled thermonuclear reaction system, are limited in the amount of thrust they can produce, thus they can be used only in space. Among the propulsion systems with specific impulse in the thousands, only the pulsed fission and the pulsed fusion systems are capable of commuting between space and the surface of celestial bodies.   K. A. E.

SEE ALSO: FUEL, ROCKET, ROCKET ENGINE, SPACE VEHICLES

This liquid-fueled sled, used for testing missile components, travels at 920 miles (1,480 kilometers) per hour.

Rocket sled Rocket sleds are vehicles used for testing materials and equipment designed for high speed flight. Test animals and humans also ride the sleds. This is part of aeromedical research to learn more about how much stress and strain the human body can stand.

Clusters of rockets are mounted on the rear of the rocket sled to propel it at great speeds down a railroad type track. Cameras, tape recorders, radio and other electronic equipment inform the scientists and engineers of what takes place during the high-speed test run.

Rocket sleds were developed as an inexpensive and practical way to conduct research and development testing of complex and inexpensive components used in high-performance AIRCRAFT, MISSILES and SPACE VEHICLES. Conditions simulating the dynamic forces of high-speed flight are created. Scientists program the desired acceleration and track speed of the sled

by varying the size, number and firing sequence of the *solid propellant rockets* used to power the sled. Occasionally *liquid fueled rocket* boosters are used when more precise control of the power source thrust is desired. ACCELERATION forces as high as 25G (25 times the normal force of GRAVITY) have been achieved. Track speeds approaching 4 times the speed of sound or about 3,000 miles (4,828 kilometers) per hour have been programmed.

Controlled deceleration of the rocket sled is accomplished by air, water, or mechanical braking. A frequently-used technique is to fill a concrete trough between the rails with varying levels of water held in position by portable dams which are easily penetrated. A water-scoop mounted beneath the sled plows into the water with a tremendous braking effect. Deceleration forces well in excess of 100 G's may be created.

The nature of the test determines the shape of the rocket sled. It may be the nose section of an aircraft or just a basic platform with equipment mounted on it.

The test track has continuously welded precision steel rails which are very accurately laid. The long track at Holloman Air Force Base, New Mexico, is 35,000 feet (1,050 meters) long while others are much shorter. Special slippers on the bottom of the sled grip the rails to prevent it from leaving the track during the test run.

Rocket sled tests vary considerably in purpose. A few of these include: external force loadings are applied to materials and structures; stability testing of airfoil and aerodynamic shapes; simulated rain erosion tests on radomes, etc.; testing of aircraft escape mechanisms; study of extremes forces upon missile instrumentation and components; evaluation of new protective measures for the human body in flight.

Since the duration of a test run is only seconds it is necessary to employ instrumentation both on the sled and along the track to provide detailed information on what occurred during the test. Radio telemetry, recorders, high speed cameras, and other devices provide information which is later studied by the engineers and scientists. Frequently, electronic computers are used to assist in the interpretation and evaluation of this test information.   R.J.J.

SEE ALSO: INERTIA, ROCKET, ROCKET ENGINE, SOUND, STRESS

Rock collecting equipment: magnifier, rock hammer, pencil, hardness set, test-fluids and streak plate

Granite, one of the most common rocks, has crystals of quartz, feldspar, and mica minerals contained in it

Rocks Rocks are a mixture of two or more minerals. They make up most of the crust of earth and are the source of soil. Rocks provide people with many different types of important building materials.

Geologists put all rocks into three great groups: *igneous, sedimentary,* or *metamorphic* rocks. Common rocks of these three classes are: granite, basalt, pumice, obsidian, sandstone, shale, limestone; slate, schist, gneiss, marble and quartzite.

A rock may be composed of several types of minerals. Where this occurs, it is usually possible to see and identify the individual types within a single specimen. Most rocks are made up of minerals. The minerals in the rock are not chemically combined and as a result they retain their original characteristics.

IGNEOUS ROCKS

Igneous rocks were once hot and fluid, a sort of "mineral soup" that geologists call *magma.* If this molten rock cools slowly within the earth, the minerals contained in it will have time to form large crystals, just as hot fudge, if cooled slowly, sugars. The more slowly it cools, the larger are the crystals. Granite, pegmatite, and gabbro are examples of igneous rock cooled slowly within the earth. Felsite and basalt, composed of tiny crystals as fine or finer than granulated sugar, cooled more rapidly either within the earth or as a lava that flowed from a volcano. The surface of volcanic lava cools so rapidly that it is glassy, just as fudge cooled rapidly is smooth and creamy. Pumice, with its trapped gas bubbles, and glassy obsidian are rocks of this type.

The most common igneous rocks and a few of their identifying features are:

Granite: Granite always contains the minerals QUARTZ (usually colorless to smoky) and FELDSPAR (pink or white). It also usually contains either mica (black or white) or hornblende (dark green to black). The mineral grains vary in size from those about ⅛ inch (3.2 millimeters) across to those are large as one's finger.

Pegmatite: Pegmatite is a coarse granite containing grains from as large as a person's thumb to those as large or larger than a piano.

Felsite: Felsite is a fine-grained, light colored igneous rock with mineral crystals almost too small to be recognizable without a magnifying glass. It may or may not contain pnenocrysts like porphyry rocks.

Basalt: Balsalt is a fine-grained, very dark-colored igneous rock. It is often referred to as *tap rock.*

Porphyry: Porphyry is a rock containing large crystals of one or more minerals embedded in a matrix of fine grained rock. Porphyry rocks are indicators that the rock had been subjected to two stages of cooling, once relatively fast and the other slower.

SEDIMENTARY ROCKS

Sedimentary rocks are formed from the sediments that come from the weathering and erosion of other rocks. These sediments may be of *igneous* or *metamorphic* rock origin. They may also come from other sedimentary rocks that have been worn down. Some sediments come from the remains of plants and animals. Sedimentary rocks are often divided into groups on the basis of the type of sediment in their composition. *Mechanical sediments* are fragments of other rocks. *Organic sediments* are

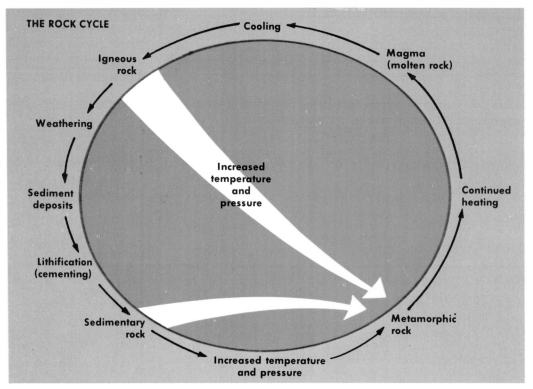

THE ROCK CYCLE

Cooling

Igneous rock

Magma (molten rock)

Weathering

Increased temperature and pressure

Continued heating

Sediment deposits

Lithification (cementing)

Sedimentary rock

Metamorphic rock

Increased temperature and pressure

The rock cycle shows that any form of rock passed through specific conditions that created that form.

the remains of plants and animals such as ferns and shells. *Chemical sediments* are various minerals that were, at one time, dissolved in water. Examples are gypsum and common rock salt. Most types of sediment were carried and deposited by water. Because of this, sedimentary rocks were formed in horizontal layers, or *strata*. These are called *stratified* rocks. There are many land areas that are high above sea level. Deep under the surface there are layers of sedimentary rock. At one time these land areas were under a shallow, inland sea.

The most common sedimentary rocks and a few of their identifying features are:

Shale: Shale is composed of CLAY sediments. This clay is often made of the mineral *kaolin*. Shale is found in thin layers which, when exposed at the surface, weathers rapidly. It is fairly soft and can be easily broken. It is of little economic use to man.

Sandstone: Sandstone has a rough, gritty texture like sandpaper and is formed by the cementing of particles of sand. It occurs in layers and breaks into flat slabs. Sandstone, being porous, may contain considerable moisture.

Conglomerate: Conglomerate is a mixture of sand and pebbles cemented together and sometimes called *pudding stone*.

Limestone: Limestone is made of precipitated CALCIUM CARBONATE or of fine to coarsely ground sea shells and corals cemented together. It is a soft rock, and a scratch by nail or knife leaves a broad white streak. If a drop of dilute hydrochloric acid is placed on a clean, freshly scraped surface, foamy bubbles of escaping carbon dioxide gas will form. Sometimes small fossil shell animals are seen in it.

METAMORPHIC ROCKS

Metamorphic rocks are rocks that have been altered by tremendous pressures and heat. They differ from igneous rocks, whose crystals are mixed, by having the crystals of each mineral more or less lined up in bands or layers. They differ from sedimentary rocks, which may also have a layered appearance, being much harder and crystalline. These are not gritty as sandstone is. Common types are schist, gneiss, slate, quartzite and marble.

Listed below are the most common metamorphic rocks and their identifying features.

Gneiss: Gneiss resembles granite but has a banded appearance caused by the lining-up of mineral crystals. It is formed by the alteration of granite, or other rocks with sufficiently varied compositions.

Schist: Schist is like gneiss, but contains

IGNEOUS ROCKS

OBSIDIAN

PORPHYRY

BASALT

INTRUSIVE ROCK

GRANITE

PUMICE

GRANITE

SYENITE

GABBRO

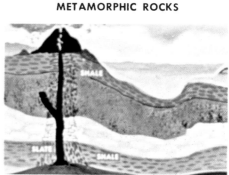

Courtesy Society For Visual Education, Inc.

SEDIMENTARY ROCKS

CONGLOMERATE

LIMESTONE WHICH
SOMETIMES CONTAINS
FOSSILS

METAMORPHIC ROCKS

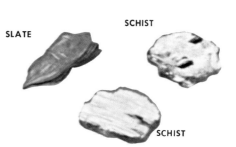

SLATE IS MADE FROM SHALE BY HEAT AND
ROCKS WITHIN THE EARTH

GRAY

SANDSTONE

SLATE

SCHIST

SCHIST

YELLOW

RED

SLATE

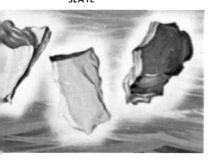

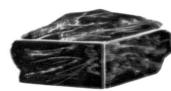

MARBLE

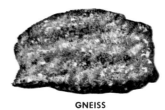

GNEISS

more mica or other dark minerals. Its bands appear as much more complete layers than those of gneiss and may be almost paper thin.

Quartzite: Quartzite has a granular, sugary appearance not unlike sandstone but has a firm, smooth texture, because when it was broken, the fracture went through the sand grains. It is very hard and difficult to break. It is a metamorphic sandstone.

Slate: Slate resembles shale but is hard and does not crumble or break easily in the fingers as does shale, which splits in a direction parallel to its natural bedding. The cleavage of slate bears no relation to the natural bedding and may even be at right angles to it.

Marble: Marble is a recrystallized limestone and has a coarse grain. It can be scratched by a knife but not as easily as limestone. It will also foam when a drop of acid is applied to a clean scraped surface.

All rocks exposed to the earth's surface are gradually eroded by the action of heat, cold, rain, snow, and ice. This eroding process is called *weathering*. It greatly alters the appearance of a rock, softens it, and changes its texture. Since all exposed surfaces of rocks are somewhat weathered, a fresh surface must be obtained to observe the true characteristics of the rock. A few sharp blows of a small geologic hammer will accomplish this task. The effect is quite startling. A dull, nondescript looking rock opens to display a colorful, sparkling, beautiful interior hidden beneath its surface,

In weathering, a rock's surface is expanded by the sun's heat, while cold causes it to contract. A rock does not expand and contract as a unit, since various minerals composing it differ in their degree of expansion and contraction. As a result, the rock begins to crack. Water seeps into the cracks and when it freezes, it widens the cracks. Water is a great solvent, too, and may carry off some of the mineral constituents of the rock in solution. In time, fragments of rocks are broken off and later become smaller fragments, eventually small enough for rains to carry off to streams and rivers.

There are many other ways that rocks weather, including wind, glaciers, pressures within the earth called uplifting, and destructive breakdown by plant roots.   V. V. N.

SEE ALSO: GEOLOGY, HARDNESS SCALE

Rocky Mountains see North America

James P. Rowan

Squirrels, like all rodents, like to gnaw constantly.

Rodentia (Rodent) A rodent is a kind of mammal. Most rodents are small creatures, such as the squirrels, chipmunks, and mice. Beavers and porcupines are larger. Rodents have large front gnawing teeth. *Rodent* is from the Latin word for "gnawing."

Rodents live for the most part on vegetable types of food, especially grains or nuts. Their teeth are unusually well adapted to eating and gnawing hard objects. They have two wedge-shaped incisors in both the upper and lower jaws. These teeth keep growing from the base to compensate for the wearing away brought about by gnawing activities. Only the front parts of these teeth have enamel. Thus the backs are less protected and wear faster. This brings about a continuously sharpened set of front teeth.

Other useful adaptions in rodents are the strong claws useful for climbing or digging. In the beaver, webbed hind feet and the broad tail are characteristics that make it an adept swimmer.

Other rodents include the gophers or ground squirrels, woodchucks or "groundhogs," chinchillas, and cavies. A South American animal called the *capybara* is the largest rodent, sometimes growing to 4 feet (1.2 meters) in size.

Rodents live in various habitats throughout the world. Gophers and prairie dogs are burrowers, making long underground passages. Field mice live in various places, but as their name suggests, often in fields or grassy areas where their small nests amidst the grass may be quite concealed. Squirrels tend to nest in hollow parts of trees. Beavers and muskrats live near water. The beaver makes a most ingenious nest of branches in

SOME RODENT CHARACTERISTICS

Rodents have a variety of fur textures, from the soft fur of the chinchilla, used to make coats, to the almost spiny hair of the rat.

Rodents have wedge-shaped incisors that grow from their base to make up for the wearing away that is the result of their constant gnawing.

Rodents have strong claws that are used for digging or climbing. The beaver paw shows long, sharp claws that help it dig its lodges.

Photo courtesy Society for Visual Aids, Inc.

The South American Capybara is the largest rodent.

Macmillan Science Company

The pack rat collects shiny objects.

White mice are bred as laboratory animals.

Daniel Oldfield

a stream, the top of which rises like a dome from the water. Underwater entrances lead to passages above the water level where the nest is snug and dry.

Rodents have the largest number of species of all the mammalian orders. The RAT is often regarded as the worst pest of all animals. Rodents as a group are destructive. CHIPMUNKS and squirrels are companionable though sometimes they bite. They serve us usefully by often ''losing'' acorns which helps distribute this seed.

The *jerboa* or kangaroo rat of North Africa and Asia travels like a kangaroo. It is mouse-like, with strong hind legs and an 8-inch (20.3-centimeter) tail, used in moving from place to place. In the woods of North America is found the *pack rat,* with long hair and a bushy tail. This rodent will pick up and carry to its nest any object that is interesting or shiny. Because it sometimes sees something more interesting than the first item it is carrying, and drops one item to pick up another, it has earned the name of *trader rat.*   D.J.I.

SEE ALSO: BEAVER, MAMMALIA, MOUSE, PORCU-PINE, PRAIRIE DOG, SQUIRREL

Rods and cones see Eye

Roe (ROH) Roe are fish eggs, or spawn, massed within the ovary of a female fish. The term *roe* also refers to the species of small deer of Asia and Europe. The robuck has rough horns about a foot (.3 meter) long, usually with 3 tines.

Roentgen, Wilhelm Konrad (RENT-guhn) (1845-1923) Wilhelm Roentgen was a German physicist who discovered X-rays. At first it was called the *Roentgen ray,* but later was universally known as the X-ray because of its unknown nature. In 1901, he received the first NOBEL PRIZE in Physics for his work.

Wilhelm Roentgen was born at Lennep, Prussia, on March 27, 1845. He began his education in the Netherlands, and later attended the University of Zurich. After lecturing and teaching at the universities of Würzburg and Strasbourg, he became Director of the Physical Institute at Giessen in 1879. In 1885 he returned to Würzburg as professor of physics, and it was there that he discovered, quite by accident, the new X-ray.

While experimenting with a glass tube from which the air had been pumped, Roentgen happened to pass an electric current through the tube. Nearby was a screen coated with barium platinocyanide. Suddenly he noticed that the screen was glowing with a greenish-blue light. Experimenting with this radiation coming from the evacuated glass tube, Roentgen discovered that radiation would pass through many substances of varying densities placed between the tube and the screen. He named these rays "X-rays," and presented his discovery to the Physico-Medical Society of Würzburg in November of 1895.

Roentgen also conducted research in elasticity, conduction of heat in crystals, and the ratio of the specific heats of gases.   D. H. J.
SEE ALSO: RADIATION, X-RAY

Roller bearing see Bearing

Rook see Crow

Root The root is the part of the plant that usually grows down into the soil. Roots have two main jobs: (1) anchoring the plant to the ground; (2) absorbing water and salts from the soil and conducting them up to the STEM. Roots lack the green coloring, chlorophyll. Some roots store food. Others can reproduce new plants.

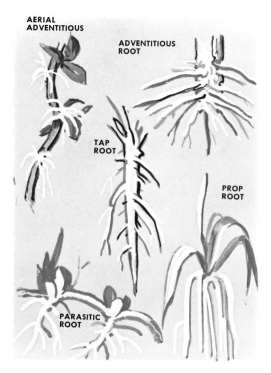

AERIAL ADVENTITIOUS
ADVENTITIOUS ROOT
TAP ROOT
PROP ROOT
PARASITIC ROOT

There are three kinds of roots. The *primary* root is the first root of a baby plant or *embryo*. It develops directly from the seed. Secondary roots are all those that branch out from the primary root. Any root which develops from any part of the plant other than the first root is called *adventitious*. The prop roots of corn is an example. PROPAGATION of plant parts produces adventitious roots.

There are two types of root systems. If the primary root grows longer and larger than all the others, it is a taproot. Dandelions, carrots, and many trees have this kind of system. If the plant grows many adventitious roots and the primary root is no longer conspicuous, it is called a *fibrous* or *diffuse* root system. Grasses and cereal grains have this kind of system.

Roots are called annuals if they live for one year. Biennal roots live two years. If the roots live more than two years, they are called perennials.

Some plants have air or *aerial* roots. They absorb water and minerals from rain. Vanilla orchid has this type. In rare cases, roots may even develop chlorophyll and make food. Climbing roots of English ivy are a form of air roots. Roots of such parasites as dodder and mistletoe grow into the vascular tissue of trees to get needed materials.

It is not clearly understood how roots absorb water. For a long time, it was believed that OSMOSIS was the prime process. Now there is evidence that the rate of respiration affects absorption. All roots need oxygen to carry on respiration. The amount of air in soil is as important as the amount of water. Most plants will die if their roots are always in water. However, a few—paddy rice and willow—thrive on it.

INTERNAL STRUCTURE

Each root tip has four distinct areas. The very end of a tiny root is covered with cells called the *root cap.* Just in back of this area is the *meristem,* the cells which are constantly dividing, enabling the root to grow in length. The root cap protects this delicate area. As the root pushes deeper into the soil, root-cap cells get worn away and must be replaced. Cells produced in the growing region are left behind and begin to lengthen, taking on the shape of the tissue it is destined to become. This is the area of *elongation.* The fourth region is the *maturation* or root-hair zone. Here cells have matured and become phloem tubes, xylem vessels, parenchyma cells, and others. Epidermal cells send out projections called *root hairs.* One rye plant has billions of root hairs. These increase the area of absorption. The four zones of the root tip advance downward into the soil, leaving the older part of the root behind.

The internal structure of an older root is similar to that of an older stem; it produces a corky bark on the outside. The vascular cambium produces layers of phloem and xylem cells each year. Probably the biggest difference is the origin of branches or secondary roots. These develop just inside the endodermis from the pericycle. They push through the cortex and epidermal layer.

Root pressure is one factor that helps water get to tops of trees. Under good conditions, this pressure can push a column of water up 60 feet (18.3 meters). The direction and growth of roots depend on heredity, gravity, amount of water, oxygen, minerals, and soil temperatures.   H.J.C.

SEE ALSO: PLANT TISSUE, TRANSPLANTING

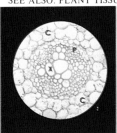

Cross-section of a root shows the xylem, or conducting cells (X); the phloem, or food-transporting cells (P); and the cortex, or outer cells (C).

Photomicrograph courtesy of National Teaching Aids, Inc.

Rootworm This is the name for a number of different insect larva that harm garden and farm crops. They are parasites and do millions of dollars of damage every year.

Rootworms can be the larvae of white-fringed beetles, and feed on strawberry, peanut, and cotton plants. The rootworm or larvae of the cucumber beetle chews the roots of squash, melons, and cucumbers. The grub feeds for a month before forming the pupa. The corn rootworm is very difficult to destroy. Crop rotation and insecticides can reduce infestation.

Rootworm is also the name for several roundworms in the nematode group.   H.J.C.

Rope A Rope is a strong, thick cord. Ropes are commonly made by twisting or braiding such material as thin wires, leather strips, or strands of fibers (FLAX, HEMP). Sometimes ropes are saturated with oil or tar to increase their strength.

SEE: ECONOMIC BOTANY

Rose Rosebushes, shrubs, and trees range from 1 to 20 feet (.3 to 6.1 meters) high. FLOWERS come in many colors except blue and black. The oil in the petals gives roses a pleasant odor.

Rose LEAVES are arranged alternately on a prickly STEM. The perfect flowers have five petals or multiples of five. The essential oils in the petals evaporate into the air. Fixed oils in some plants do not do this. It takes over a 1,000 pounds (454 kilograms) of flowers to make one ounce (28 grams) of concentrated oil called *otto* of roses. The FRUIT or rose hip is a fleshy *torus,* the enlarged receptacle plus the ovary. It contains several achenes.

Horticulturists are constantly developing new varieties of roses. Hybrid tea roses are the most important commercial kind today. Ramblers are small-flowered climbers. The American Beauty, symbolic flower of the District of Columbia, is a member of the hybrid perpetuals. Floribundas, a new group, have hardy, long-blooming clusters of double flowers.

Propagation of roses is done by grafting, budding, or cutting back. In this latter

Pink roses

F. A. Blashfield

Courtesy Society For Visual Education, Inc.

Tea rose

method, ROOTS develop *adventitious* buds (not originating from the primary root). These grow into new shoots. Often cultivated roses are grafted to the roots of wild roses because the underground system of the latter is far superior.

The rose family, Rosaceae, includes such plants as blackberries and cherries. Enemies of roses are aphids, Japanese beetles, midges, rose bugs, and red spiders. Black spot and mildew are fungi diseases. H.J.C.

Rosemary Rosemary is an evergreen shrub about 6 feet (1.8 meters) tall. The LEAVES have a sweet scent. They are shiny and dark-green above but whitish on the underside.

Small FLOWERS grow in clusters and are light blue in color. They are perfect, having both male and female parts. Five sepals are united around five irregular petals. The pistil is formed of two united, bilobed carpels. When this matures into a FRUIT, each carpel becomes a one-seeded, bony nutlet.

Aromatic leaves are used as seasoning.

Rosemary

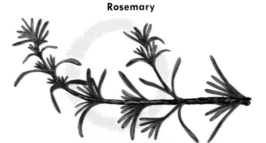

Distillation of leaves produces an oil used in some medicines. Rosemary belongs to the mint or Lamiaceae family. H. J. C.

Rose-of-Sharon It is a hardy shrub, sometimes called *shrubby Althea.* It grows 5 to 15 feet (1.5 to 4.6 meters) tall and has leaves about 4 inches (10 centimeters) long. The leaves, which are sometimes several colors, are oval and have sharply-toothed edges.

Rose-of-Sharon blooms during the early fall. It has single or double bell-shaped flowers in shades of red, purple, violet, or white. A column in the center of the flower is white, while the center itself is usually red.

The Rose-of-Sharon (*Hibiscus syriacus*) thrives in well-drained soil. It is valued in the home garden as a late-blooming shrub; and its flowers are most appreciated on dark or gloomy days. It is a member of the MALLOW family. M. R. L.

SEE ALSO: SHRUBS

Rosewood Rosewood is the center or HEARTWOOD part of a tree trunk. The wood is usually dark in color and very hard. Several kinds of tropical trees produce rosewood.

Brazilian rosewood is the most widely used rosewood. Its wood is purplish-black, dense, and often striped. The grain is coarse and even. Many scientific instruments, fine cabinets, and sporting goods are made from this wood.

Burmese rosewood or padauk is red with black stripes. Its hardness makes it suitable for furniture, as it can be highly polished. It is also used for veneer and for constructing certain parts of automobiles.

Rosewood belongs to the Leguminosae family. It differs from this group in one characteristic: the FRUIT or LEGUME is modified, forming a pod which does not *dehisce* or open when it is ripe. H. J. C.

SEE: HEARTWOOD

Ross, Sir Ronald (1857-1932) Ross, a British physician and bacteriologist, won the 1902 NOBEL PRIZE for physiology and medicine for his malaria research. He was the first to prove that mosquitos carry malaria parasites.

Sir Ross's research began in 1892, when malaria was believed to be caused by the foul air associated with swamps. Some research indicated that malaria had its basis in a parasitic protozoa and was probably spread by mosquitos. Ross was able to show that the malarial parasite did pass part of its life cycle in mosquitos. The female mosquitos picked up the parasite by sucking blood from an infected person and then passing it on to any other person it bit. Through his work Ross showed that a disease can be wiped out by eliminating the insect that transmits it.   P.P.S.

Rot Rotting is the breaking down of plant or animal cells by living things. This process is both good and bad. If all the dead leaves, logs, and animals in the woods did not rot, the earth would be piled high with them.

PARASITES and SAPROPHYTES cause things to rot. Certain of these bacteria, fungi, and viruses can do great damage to tissues. There are two forms of rot. *Fermentation* is the decay of organic materials, usually carbohydrates, in the absence of free oxygen. *Putrefaction* is usually the breakdown of proteins inside large organisms where little or no oxygen is available. This often yields a foul smell.

Adverse environmental factors, insects, or worms can break down cell walls. Rot can then begin because parasites can enter and start to feed upon live tissue.

Man deliberately lets certain things rot or ferment in order to produce various industrial products. Chemical changes occur in rotting which reduce complex molecules to simpler ones. Bacteria are used in septic tanks, cesspools, and sewage plants. H. J. C.
SEE ALSO: BACTERIA, BOTANY, FUNGUS, PLANT DISEASE, PLANT PESTS

Rotation The movement of the earth as it turns on its axis is called rotation. The earth rotates, or spins, as it travels in its path (revolution) around the sun. As the earth rotates, one of its halves is turned toward the sun and receives light; as the earth turns, daylight fades and darkness, or night,

comes. The earth turns completely around in 24 hours. Thus DAY AND NIGHT combined total 24 hours. As the earth moves in its orbit around the sun, it also tilts on its axis; this "tilting" causes changes in the earth's position which result in the seasons. The movement of the earth around the sun takes one year.

PTOLEMY, who lived about 150 A.D., believed that Earth did not rotate. For fourteen hundred years his idea predominated. Later, some men came to believe the earth did rotate; and in 1851, Jean Foucault, a French physicist, performed an experiment at the Pantheon in Paris, using a long pendulum and a ring of sand, which demonstrated that the earth was turning.   E. M. N.
SEE ALSO: CENTRIFUGAL AND CENTRIPETAL FORCES, EARTH, PENDULUM

Rotifera (roh-TIFF-er-uh) These delightful, tiny animals are called "wheel bearers." They do not have real wheels, of course; but around the mouth, there are two wide lobes or folds of cells covered with tiny cilia which look like small hairs. When the rotifer swims or eats, the cilia beat very fast; and the lobes seem to turn like wheels.

The animals in this large group have interesting shapes. Many are round like bubbles. Some are shaped like flowers on a tall stem. Others look like worms with crowns of feathers. All are less than 1/50 of an inch (.5 millimeter) long and may be seen only under a microscope.

Rotifers prefer the fresh water of ponds and lakes, though a few live in the ocean. While some float, most rotifers live on shore bottoms or attached to plants on the edge of the shore. Others are able to live in the moss of rain gutters, roofs, and tree bark. Many are parasites which live on the bodies of other animals such as worms, protozoa, and snails.

Movement from place to place is inter-

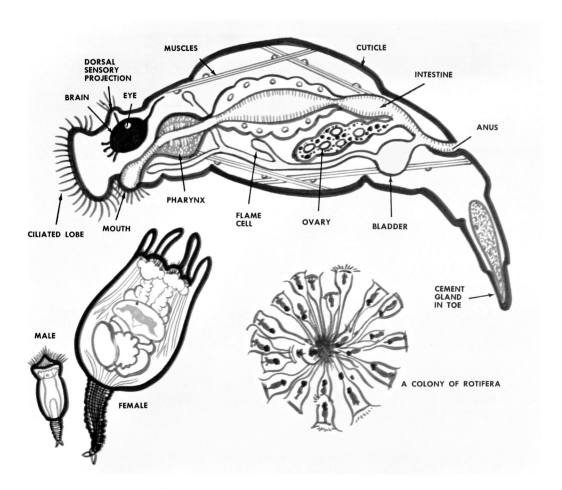

MUSCLES · CUTICLE · DORSAL SENSORY PROJECTION · INTESTINE · BRAIN · EYE · ANUS · PHARYNX · FLAME CELL · OVARY · BLADDER · MOUTH · CILIATED LOBE · CEMENT GLAND IN TOE · MALE · FEMALE · A COLONY OF ROTIFERA

esting to watch. The cilia, which form a crown around the mouth, are used for feeding and swimming. When they beat rapidly, they either propel the rotifer through the water or draw food to the mouth. The hind end of the body tapers to form a tail, or foot, which ends in two pointed "toes." Actually these toes open into glands which secrete a sticky substance. During feeding, the rotifer cements its body to a solid surface by means of the toes. While the rotifer is swimming, the foot acts as a rudder.

The body of a rotifer resembles a tiny, glass fish bowl. The thin body wall is transparent, so that the inner body workings may be seen. Behind the mouth there is a unique grinding organ, called the *mastax*. It contains many hard plates, operated by powerful muscles, and is used for grinding food. The mastax opens into a straight, hollow intestine which ends above the foot at the anus.

The rotifer has an amazing ability to protect itself against unfavorable living con-

ditions. Its body gradually dries, shrinks, and becomes wrinkled. In this state, it is able to survive for months or years under temperatures which would kill most animals. When the body is moistened, the rotifer is able to return to normal activity.

These animals have bodies made of many cells. As the rotifer grows into an adult, however, the cell membranes disappear; and the body becomes a large mass of protoplasm containing the nuclei from the cells. A definite number of nuclei, between 900 and 1000, are present for each species.

Reproduction is mainly asexual. In the spring, the female may produce several generations of offspring. These large eggs develop into adults without being fertilized. In the fall, sexual reproduction may occur, since a few of these small eggs are produced which hatch into males. In some species no males have been found.   E. P. L.

SEE ALSO: ANIMALS, CLASSIFICATION OF

Rotogravure see Printing

Rotor A rotor is the rotating, or turning, part of certain MACHINERY. In a turbine, the wheel-like rotor contains the blades which the water or steam act on. The wheel turns, turning the shaft and driving the generator. In a helicopter, the rotors are propellers which lift the helicopter into the air and help steer it. The helicopter rotors are turned by the engine.

Roundworm see Ascaris, Nemathelminthes

Rubber Rubber is the material which has the wonderful ability to stretch and return to its original shape over and over again. It is used for rubber bands, elastic bandages, tires, and other materials where continuous flexibility is needed. It also is an excellent insulating material for electricity. New plastics have replaced rubber for some purposes.

Columbus saw Haitian children playing with black rubber balls made from the juice of the *hevea tree*. This tree is a tropical tree and can grow only within 10° of the equator, and is the source of 99 per cent of the world's supply of natural rubber. The *gauvale shrub* has been cultivated as a "rubber plant," but is not used extensively. This plant must be cut off to obtain the juices, whereas the hevea tree can be tapped over and over for as many as thirty years.

Perhaps the English scientist, Joseph Priestley, who gave rubber its name, put this stretchy substance to its first practical use when he discovered that a piece would erase pencil marks. But early rubber was sticky in summer and hard in winter. It had little actual practical value until Charles Goodyear, an American inventor, accidentally found that with the addition of sulfur and heat, crude rubber lost the usual qualities and remained soft, nonsticky, and resiliently pliable. This process became known as *vulcanization*. The discovery made possible wide use of the substance.

Rubber is made from a milky juice called *latex* (from the Latin word for "milk," which it resembles). Slashes are made daily

Phyllis Neulist

Above: Tapping of a rubber tree. Below: Two ways of processing rubber

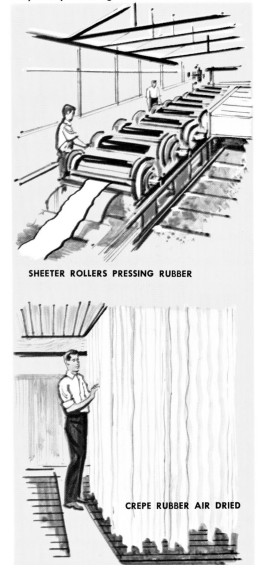

SHEETER ROLLERS PRESSING RUBBER

CREPE RUBBER AIR DRIED

in the trees (they heal quickly), and about an ounce (30 milliliters) of latex is collected. Rubber is separated and evaporated from the liquid part of the latex. Three methods are used. The best of the three methods is *smoking.* A wooden paddle is dipped in latex and held over a little fire which dries it, leaving a thin layer of rubber. By repeating this procedure many times, a ball called a "biscuit" is built up, cut off, and processed. A second method, *coagulation,* consists of adding acetic acid and water to latex. In a few hours the rubber thickens by stages into a sheet separated from the fluid; it is cleaned and processed. *Spraying* is a process in which latex trickles onto a fast-spinning plate. Liquids fly out, but the rubber remains, dried by warm air. It flakes off into containers alongside. This method produces the cleanest, toughest product.

The final steps of preparation include cleaning and the addition of chemicals to harden and strengthen, or vulcanize, it. Rolling and molding by pressure and heat create the final rubber products.

Though at first Brazil was the sole producer of rubber, the British early planted rubber trees throughout their Eastern and African possessions.

Today, Akron, Ohio, is the largest rubber-processing city.   D.J.I.

SEE ALSO: ELASTICITY

Rubber, synthetic Rubber has changed greatly since Columbus' time when it was used only for toy balls. Much rubber is now made in laboratories instead of from the rubber tree.

MICHAEL FARADAY found its chemical

SOME SYNTHETIC RUBBERS	
Buna N (Nitrile)	Resists heat, wear and tear, aging, and oil; used in hoses and machine parts that need to be oil-resistant.
Butyl	Does not permit gases or air to go through it; used for inner tubes and radiator hoses.
Polysulphide (Thiokol)	Resists oils, solvents, and air; used for gaskets, gasoline hoses, and printing rollers.
Neoprene	Weather- and chemical-resistant; used to cover wire and cable.
Silicone	Resists heat and cold very well; used in machine parts that require heat resistance.
Polyurethane	Resists aging, heat, and stress; used for foam rubber products and in insulation.

components by analysis as far back as 1826. Later a man named Grenville Williams discovered *isoprene,* and in 1879 a French chemist converted isoprene into a rubber-like solid.

Until 1910 most chemists worked exclusively on isoprene rubber. When World War I cut the Germans off from natural rubber, they experimented and produced *methyl rubber* in the first synthetic rubber factory. After the war, chemists gave up making synthetic rubber, since natural rubber was very cheap.

The importance of natural rubber was realized during World War II. Rubber is grown only in tropical areas; once these sources were cut off because of the war, nations grew desperate. One of the ways they adjusted to the rubber shortage was to develop *synthetic* rubber. A rubber-like compound called *Buna S.,* first developed in Germany, was made from raw materials obtained from coal or petroleum. The United States began producing synthetic rubber with the development of Neoprene. Since then newer synthetic rubbers have been developed for their own specific qualities such as resistance to acid or abrasion.   P.P.S.

SEE ALSO: PLASTICS

Rubber plant The rubber plant is often grown as a house plant because it lives year after year. The LEAVES of a rubber plant are a dark, glossy green on top. The underside is duller. The sturdy upright STEM may be 9 feet (2.7 meters) tall after only four years of growth.

The alternate leaves of this perennial grow 3-12 inches (7.6-30.5 centimeters) long. Lower leaves die and drop off first. The rubber plant produces a mass of small FLOWERS in the form of a dense head. Flowers lack petals and are either pistillate or staminate. The hollowed-out receptacle and tiny ovaries mature into a multiple FRUIT. Each ovary forms a nutlet with one seed.

The rubber plant is a close relative of the fig. It belongs to the mulberry or Moraceae family. Its enemies include scale insects and mealy bugs. Propagation may be done by cuttings or *air layering.*   H.J.C.

Synthetic ruby

Rubella see Measles

Rubidium (roo-BIDD-ee-um) Rubidium is a rare metallic element of the alkali family. The free element is not found in nature but must be freed from its natural salts by electrical treatment. Its name was derived from the Latin word meaning "red" because rubidium gives a red flame.

Rubidium, along with cesium, was discovered in 1861 when Robert Bunsen and Gustav Kirchhoff were testing German mineral water with a spectroscope. They noted a distinct, new-type red flame line; and later they isolated the new element, rubidium, which gave these new spectrum lines.

Rubidium (symbol Rb) has atomic number 37. Its atomic weight is 85.47. It forms salts much like the other alkali metals. D.A.B.

SEE ALSO: ATOM, ELEMENTS

Rubidium-strontium dating method

The rubidium-strontium method is a technique used by geologists to measure the ages of rocks and minerals. It is based on the principle that rubidium-87 decays at a specific rate to produce strontium-87, and is a measure of time.

The rubidium-strontium dating technique is one of several methods to measure *radioactive* decay rates. The age of a specimen can be determined from calculations of the measured ratio of the daughter *isotope* strontium-87 to the parent *isotope* rubidium-87. Knowing the HALF-LIFE of this radioactive decay sequence and using a *mass spectrometer,* the age determinations are then made possible. One of the problems with this method is in determining the amount of "common" strontium-87 present, as compared to the amount of *radiogenic* strontium-87.

The Rb-Sr method is principally used to study the age and origin of *meteorites* and the oldest earth rocks. It is most effective when dealing with materials with a large Rb/Sr ratio. Minerals containing *potassium,* among them *biotite, muscovite,* and the potassium *feldspars,* are used.   P.P.S.

SEE ALSO: HALF LIFE, RADIOACTIVITY

Ruby The ruby is one of the hardest of GEMS. Some may be more costly than diamonds. The best rubies are found in Burma. Some are called *pigeon-blood* rubies because their deep red color is tinged with blue. Rubies are found in other countries of southern Asia and in the United States.

Rubies and sapphires are made of *aluminum oxide,* and are similar to the common mineral form, *corundum.* Tiny quantities of chromium and titanium produce the difference in color. Rubies and sapphires are among the rarest of gemstones. A distinct starlike pattern is produced in some stones by the dispersion of light about the six-fold axis of the mineral's crystal. These are very precious.   J.A.D./P.P.S.

Ruffed grouse see Fowl, Grouse

Ruminant (ROO-mih-nant) An animal that chews its cud and has a four-chambered stomach is called a ruminant. Sheep, goats, deer, camels, and cows are some examples of ruminants.

When food is swallowed by the animal, it passes into the *rumen* or paunch, where it is stored temporarily while the animal eats. Chewing and digestion are then carried out at leisure. The food passes from the rumen to the *reticulum,* where it is formed into small masses and elevated to the mouth to be chewed. When it is swallowed a second time it takes a different course to another chamber, the *omasum* or psalterium. It moves from there to the *abomasum.* In these last two chambers gastric digestion takes place, and the food passes to the intestine.   V. V. N.

SEE ALSO: ARTIODACTYLA

Stomach of ruminant

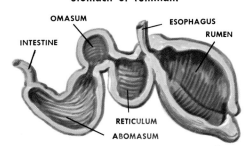

OMASUM

ESOPHAGUS

RUMEN

INTESTINE

RETICULUM

ABOMASUM

Runner

Runner A runner is a slender, trailing STEM found on a plant. Runners may take root and produce new plants wherever the leaf and bud parts come into contact with the soil. They are sometimes called *stolons*.

Runners are a form of vegetative reproduction. Ground pine, for example, sends out creeping, prostrate stems. Adventitious ROOTS grow down from each joint, or NODE. If the stem is severed between these nodes, each erect stem becomes an individual plant.

Strawberry is another herbaceous plant that develops runners. However, it produces upright stems or aerial shoots at alternate nodes. The first year a strawberry bed is laid out, the plants are spaced a foot (.3 meter) or more apart. Within 2 or 3 years the whole area is covered with runners.

Crabgrass, with profuse runners, is a pest in the lawns of many homeowners.   H.J.C.
SEE ALSO: PROPAGATION, STEM

Rupture see Hernia

Rust Rust is one of the worst plant pests. There are over 2000 kinds. They live as parasites on ferns and many seed plants. The word *rust* is the name for both the plant and the disease it causes. Some rusts need only one kind of plant to live on. Others must go from one plant to a different kind to finish their life cycle. Rust harms its host by stunting growth and reducing the fruit yield.

Rust is a fungus plant in the *Basidiomycetes* group It develops long filaments called *mycelia* which anchor it to the host plant. The club-shaped *basidium* on each mycelium produces the spores needed for reproduction. From two to five different kinds of spores are present in the life cycle.

A description of the cedar-apple rust cycle shows the alternation-of-hosts sequence. The process takes two years.

In the spring, one type of spore (*basidiospore*) is carried from the cedar tree to an apple or crabapple tree. The spores fall on the leaves and cause infected areas to appear. The yellow spots on the upper epidermis produce more spores (*spermagonial*) and the cups or pockets on the lower epidermis produce another type (*aecial*). By late summer, these spores are carried back to the red cedar. They cause growths called *cedar apples* or *galls*. *Teliospores* are produced by the next spring and then basidiospores develop within the gall through the next winter and spring. The cycle begins again when these spores reach the apple.

The greatest damage is to the apple host. The tree is stunted, the leaves begin to drop, and fruit is inferior.

The following are paired hosts of some rusts: buckthorn and oats, goldenrod and three-needled pine, barberry and wheat, Ponderosa pine and Indian paintbrush. Rusts parasitic on the Boston fern, cassava, mistletoe and mimosa do not need an alternate host.   H. J. C.
SEE ALSO: FUNGUS, PARASITE, PLANT DISEASES, SPORE FORMATION

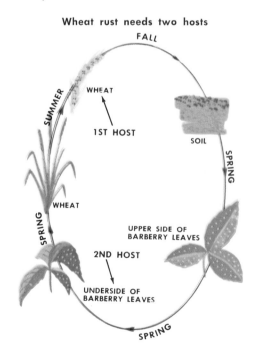

Wheat rust needs two hosts

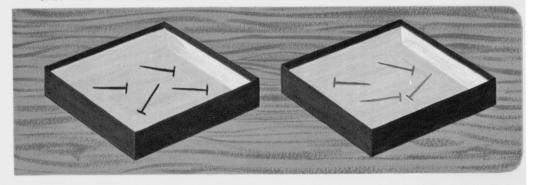
Rusting Rusting occurs when oxygen combines chemically with iron. This is most common when iron or steel is exposed to moist air. By covering the metal with paint or oil, the oxygen is prevented from reaching it.

Some steels have small amounts of other metals added to them. These metals reduce the chemical activity of the iron to the extent that either it will not rust at all (stainless steel) or it will rust only a little and stop. This second kind of steel needs no painting and has the attractive brown color typical of rust. It is used to make the exposed beams of large buildings.

Rusting is most often caused by water vapor. These tiny droplets of water contain chemically active *ionized* oxygen. The liquid adheres more closely to the steel surface than does the gaseous oxygen in air. This brings the oxygen close enough to allow it to react with the iron in the steel and form rust.

Two forms of rust exist. The first form is called *ferrous oxide* and is nearly black. This first rust will combine with more oxygen to form reddish-brown *ferric oxide*.

Rusting weakens the object on which it occurs, using up the strongly bonded iron crystals. Steel is coated with oil, paint, plastic, and other metals to prevent rusting. M. W. K.
SEE ALSO: OXIDATION, STEEL

Rutabaga (root-uh-BAY-guh) Rutabaga is an herb with a smooth, bulb-like ROOT. The large yellow taproot is eaten by both man and livestock. It is also called Swedish TURNIP or *swedes*. LEAVES and STEMS are coarse and fleshy.

Rutabagas are biennial, (the FLOWERS appear the second year of growth). Flowers form in clusters called *racemes*. Each bloom has four sepals, four yellow petals, six stamens, and one pistil of two united carpels. The dry FRUIT is classified as a silique.

These VEGETABLES are grown in the cool climates of northern countries. Since they cannot withstand frost, they are cultivated as annuals. Rutabagas belong to the mustard or Cruciferae family. H. J. C.

Rutabaga

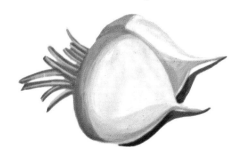

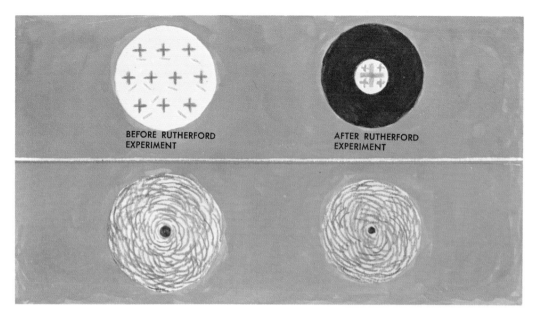

BEFORE RUTHERFORD EXPERIMENT

AFTER RUTHERFORD EXPERIMENT

Rutherford found that the mass of the atom is nearly all centered in the tiny positive nucleus, surrounded by a cloud of electrons. These electrons have a total negative charge usually equal to the positive nucleus and they differ in different elements.

Ruthenium (roo-THEE-nee-um) Ruthenium has atomic number 44, and is a metal usually found in platinum ores. In its pure state ruthenium is gray, lustrous and very hard. Because of its semiprecious nature it is used as a substitute for platinum in jewelry.

This ELEMENT was first discovered in 1828, and prepared pure in 1845. Ruthenium is insoluble in acid, as most precious metals, but it is also insoluble in the "gold solvent" *aqua regia*. In addition to its use in jewelry, ruthenium is also used to harden other metals in an alloy.

Ruthenium (symbol Ru) has atomic weight 101.07. M. S.

Rutherford, Ernest (1871-1937) Ernest Rutherford was a British physicist born in Nelson, New Zealand. He attended Canterbury College and Cambridge University. He was knighted in 1914.

In 1908 Rutherford received the Nobel Prize in chemistry for his contribution in the area of radioactivity. He discovered the actual nature and behavior of the atom. His experiments

assist present-day nuclear scientists.

As a result of observations obtained from experiments, Dr. Ernest Rutherford presented to the scientific world his concept of the atom. He said it is like a miniature solar system with a small, heavy, positively charged nucleus surrounded by fast-moving orbital electrons. He found that most of the atom, like most of our solar system, consists of empty space.

Before 1911, two theories of the atom were accepted. A man named Thompson described the atom as a sphere of positive electricity in which negative electrons are imbedded like raisins in pudding. Dr. Rutherford instead held that the positive charges in the atom form a small particle (*nucleus*) which occupies a small fraction of the total volume of the atom.

Earlier, in 1896, Henri Becquerel had discovered that the chemical element, uranium, gave off rays which could pass through matter. Soon afterward, MARIE AND PIERRE CURIE isolated other elements with the same property called RADIOACTIVITY. Rutherford pointed out that one part of the radiation from some radioactive elements was a positively-charged particle traveling at high speed. This is called an *alpha particle,* the same as the nucleus of a helium atom.

Rutherford studied other atoms by pro-

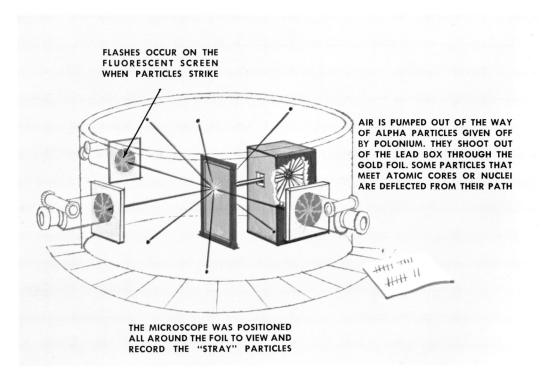

FLASHES OCCUR ON THE FLUORESCENT SCREEN WHEN PARTICLES STRIKE

AIR IS PUMPED OUT OF THE WAY OF ALPHA PARTICLES GIVEN OFF BY POLONIUM. THEY SHOOT OUT OF THE LEAD BOX THROUGH THE GOLD FOIL. SOME PARTICLES THAT MEET ATOMIC CORES OR NUCLEI ARE DEFLECTED FROM THEIR PATH

THE MICROSCOPE WAS POSITIONED ALL AROUND THE FOIL TO VIEW AND RECORD THE "STRAY" PARTICLES

jecting a beam of alpha particles through thin foils of the metal. He first used gold. With a fluorescent screen, he observed the behavior of the particles as they passed through the foil. Whenever an alpha particle struck the surface of such a fluorescent screen, a tiny flash of light appeared at the point of contact. Scientists had thought that since the alpha particles were moving rapidly, they would go right through the metal. If the positive charges and atomic mass were distributed uniformly throughout the metal, the alpha particle should not swerve too far from its original path but should go right through. Rutherford noticed that nearly all of the alpha particles that penetrated the foil had maintained their normal straight path while passing through the foil. He did observe that some were deflected through large angles, and a few were actually deflected backwards. He suggested that the alpha particles which had been scattered through large angles which were deflected probably had encountered a positively charged nucleus. Since these positively charged nuclei in the gold atoms were infrequently encountered by the alpha particles, Rutherford concluded that they must comprise a very small portion of the total volume of the atom.   J. R. S.

SEE ALSO: BOHR THEORY, NUCLEAR SCIENCE

Rye This CEREAL GRAIN has slender STEMS up to 6 feet (1.8 meters) tall. They are tough and hollow. LEAVES are grasslike and bluish in color. The seeds of rye contain large amounts of starch.

FLOWERS and FRUIT of the rye grass form an inflorescence. Many spikelets make up a single head. Each spikelet has two fertile flowers and one sterile one. The dry indehiscent fruit is classified as a caryopsis. The fruit wall is closely attached to the seed.

Rye is a minor cereal crop in the United States. The Soviet Union produces almost one half of the world's supply. Rye is used for pastureland and as a *cover crop* for soil conservation. Rye straw is used to make paper. The grain is used for cattle feed, dark bread, and alcohol. It is in the family Gramineae.   H. J. C.

SEE ALSO: CEREAL GRAINS

Rye

Saffron-producing crocus

Scarlet sage

J. W. Thompson

Saber-toothed tiger see Cat family

Sable see Weasel

Saccharin Saccharin is an organic chemical (*benzoic sulfimide*) prepared as white crystals. It is one of several sweeteners used in sugar-free diets. Though slightly bitter, it is 500 times as sweet as cane sugar, but it produces no body weight nor energy.

Sacrum see Skeleton

Saffron (SAFF-ruhn) Saffron or saffron powder is a bright yellow spice which comes from the dried stigma of the autumn crocus. The slender leaves and small white or purple flowers are well known in southern Europe, but they have been grown in America only in small garden crops.

Harvesting of saffron is not done in the United States because it is too expensive. Each crocus blossom has three saffron stigmas, and the delicate filaments must be picked by hand. It takes 75,000 hand-picked blossoms to supply enough stigmas for one pound (.5 kilogram) of saffron.

Saffron is a favorite and luxurious spice for many French, Hindustani, Italian, and Spanish recipes. J.K.K.

Safrole see Sassafras

Sage There are at least 500 varieties of sage, all members of the MINT family. Chopped or powdered, dried or fresh, sage has been used for centuries, to improve the flavor of foods, especially sausage, meats, meat dressings, fowl, fish and cheese.

The common sage, with light purple blossoms and gray-green leaves, grows about 2 feet (.6 meter) tall. Sage can grow in almost any climate of the world. J.K.K.
SEE ALSO: SPICE

Sage hen see Grouse

Sage sparrow see Finch

Sagebrush Sagebrush is a name for several kinds of shrubs that grow in dry, hot places. There are more than two hundred varieties of sagebrush and they are found in most countries.

In dry places where grass will not grow, cattle eat sagebrush. Where crops are being raised, sagebrush is harmful because it grows rapidly and takes the moisture needed for the crop. Most sagebrush grows better in poor and sandy soils than in rich ones. They bloom in summer and like warm sunshine. Some varieties grow 12 feet (3.7 meters) tall. Most have silvery leaves. M.R.L.

Sagebrush
Courtesy Society For Visual Education, Inc.

Sagittarius (sa-juh-TAIR-ee-uhs) Sagittarius is a group of stars resembling a picture of a centaur with a bow and arrow. (A centaur is a creature that is half man, half horse.) Sagittarius is sometimes called *The Archer*. This constellation lies in the southern part of the night sky during the summer. It is the ninth sign of the zodiac.

Besides the archer with his drawn bow, two other figures can also be seen in this

Sagittarius

constellation. One is a curve of stars that is called the *Milk Dipper,* which is near a thickly starred area of the Milky Way. Another group of stars in this constellation outlines a teapot. The Teapot and the Milk Dipper help to identify Sagittarius.

According to legends Sagittarius represents a famous teacher and archer named *Chieron,* who was a centaur. In the constellation his arrow points toward the constellation of the *Scorpion.*　　　C. L. K.

SEE ALSO: CONSTELLATION, SCORPIUS

Sago see Palm

Saguaro see Cactus

Sahara Desert see Africa

Saint Lawrence Seaway see North America

Saint Vitus dance Saint Vitus dance is a disease of the nervous system which causes uncontrolled muscle movements. This disease, also called *chorea,* affects twice as many girls as boys. It is most likely to occur between the ages of seven and 14.

Saint Vitus dance is caused by the same sort of infection that causes rheumatic fever. It can be recognized by the twitching of the face and jerking of the body. Attacks are most likely to happen in the spring. They go away by themselves after a few weeks, but it is best for the patient to stay in bed and to eat a good diet even if he is not very hungry. Usually the jerking gets worse if the victim is active or excited, and stops when he is asleep. The attacks may come back at intervals for a few years, but adults almost never have them.

A very similar disease occurs in dogs, called *canine chorea.* It is believed to be caused by a virus.　　　D. A. B.

Salamander (SAL-uh-man-der) Salamanders are related to frogs and toads. The tail and body have the shape of a reptile, like a lizard. Their skins are smooth and moist instead of dry and scaly. Salamanders may live in water and breathe with gills, or develop lungs and leave the water for moist land. Those on land usually return to water to lay eggs. Unlike frogs and toads, salamanders can grow new limbs and tails if the old ones are lost.

More salamanders live in North America than in any other part of the world. In the United States there are about 130 species. They live in all types of cool water, including the subterranean water in caves. Cave salamanders are light colored, and because of degenerate eyes they are blind. Their larvae have normal eyes and vision. If the larvae are bred in aquaria placed in the light, they will *metamorphose* into adults with normal eyes. Thus, loss of eyes is a response to lack of light and not an inherited adaptation.

Another interesting salamander is the *Ambystoma tigrinum* or tiger salamander. Adults are blotched with patches of olive or yellow-brown. In the southwestern part of the United States, the larvae or *axolotls* never metamorphose into adults. They breed as larvae, a condition called *neoteny.* These larvae, transferred to eastern streams, soon lose their gills and become adults.

NEWTS are less slimy than other salamanders. After hatching, they live a few

(Top) Ambystoma; (center) dusky salamander; (bottom) mud puppy

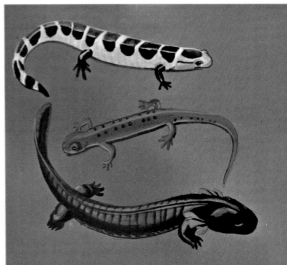

✳ THINGS TO DO

CARING FOR SALAMANDERS

1 Take a hike along a stream in damp wooded areas to look for salamanders. They appear in the open right after a rain. Carefully pick them up and place them into a box containing wet grass and soil. Be sure they are able to keep their skin moist.
2 Transfer them to a semi-aquatic terrarium. This glass house should have a saucer or a cake pan of rain water at one end and a land habitat in the rest of the terrarium. Keep a screen over the top.
3 Feed your pet small live insects and earthworms. If it does not consume any food the first few days, return it to its natural environment. Some animals simply will not adjust to a captive life.

months in water. They then lose their gills and move to land. On land they are called *efts*. In two to three years, efts return to water and change into aquatic adults. Some newts do not go through the eft stage.

The Congo eel, Amphiuma, is a 3-foot (.9-meter) salamander with small useless limbs. It lives in water but breathes with lungs. It is not a true eel, which is a type of finless fish, and should not be confused with the conger eel.

Salamander development has been extensively studied by *embryologists,* and experimental work has been done with the early stages of it.   J. C. K.
SEE ALSO: ADAPTATION, AMPHIBIAN, MARINE BIOLOGY, NEWT, ZOOLOGY

Saleratus see Sodium bicarbonate

Saliva see Salivary gland

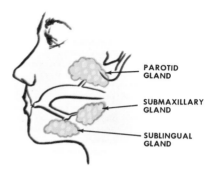

PAROTID GLAND

SUBMAXILLARY GLAND

SUBLINGUAL GLAND

Salivary glands in man

Salivary glands Salivary glands open into the mouth and make a liquid called *saliva.* Saliva moistens food and begins digestion. The saliva contains chemicals called ENZYMES to break up starchy foods (potatoes, bread) into *maltose* sugar.

The largest salivary glands are the *parotids*. These lie in the tissue below and in front of the ear. Their ducts open opposite the second molar teeth. The secretion is watery (*serous*) and contains enzymes.

The *submaxillary glands* lie below the angle of the jaw and in front of the lowest part, the parotids. Their ducts open under the tip of the tongue. They are mixed glands, forming both watery and some mucous secretions.

The smallest glands are the *sublingual*. They lie under the mucous membrane over the floor of the mouth. They are the only salivary glands not surrounded by tissue capsules. There are ten to twenty small ducts opening into the mouth. They secrete mucous.

All salivary glands are *compound glands*. In these glands there are a number of secretory endpieces opening into ducts which, in turn, empty into a common duct.   J. C. K.
SEE ALSO: DIGESTIVE SYSTEM

Salk, Jonas Edward (1914-) Dr. Salk is a famous research virologist. He led the team that discovered the killed-virus vaccine against poliomyelitis in 1954. Dr. Salk had been working on influenza viruses at the University of Pittsburgh when a national foundation asked him to try to type all the different kinds of polio. A Virus Research Laboratory was established there and the killed-virus vaccine was found in about 18 months.

The theory behind the killed-virus vaccine is that a virus, that has been killed and cannot infect or multiply, can still stimulate the body to produce antibodies against that particular VIRUS. The vaccine was thoroughly tested, first on monkeys and eventually on children (including Dr. Salk's own three children), before it was distributed nationwide.

Dr. Salk became interested in science at the College of the City of New York. After he graduated from New York University's School of Medicine, he interned at Mount Sinai Hospital.

The Salk killed-virus vaccine is the only type used in Canada and the Scandinavian countries. There polio has been virtually eliminated. In the United States another vaccine, an oral live-virus, developed by Sabin in 1961, is also used. Polio cases are still occurring in this country. Salk believes that if his vaccine were used for routine immunization, the disease could be eliminated. Further research is needed.

The Salk Institute for Biological Studies was opened in November of 1962. Salk directs its research program. One of his scientists, Roger Gullemin, received the NOBEL PRIZE for medicine in 1977. His experiments showed that the pituitary gland was controlled by secretions from the hypothalmus in the brain.   C.L.K./H.J.C.

SEE ALSO: POLIOMYELITIS, VACCINE

Salmon (SAM-uhn) Salmon are choice eating and game fish found in both the Atlantic and Pacific oceans. There are six species of Pacific salmon: the chum, sockeye, chinook, coho, pink, and little redfish. Aside from the Atlantic salmon, several other Atlantic species are popularly called trout. Trout prefer fresh water, but a few, like the steelhead, prefer the sea between SPAWNINGS. When in the sea they are silvery, but in fresh water they show the rainbow coloration.

Two main types of salmon: (top) Atlantic salmon, (bottom) king, or chinook, salmon

Both Atlantic and Pacific salmon have adipose or fatty fins on their dorsal surfaces and a spiny process at the base of the pelvic fin. The anal fins of the Atlantic species have nine rays while those from the Pacific have fourteen to seventeen rays. After spawning, the Pacific species usually die. Both eastern and western salmon are *anadromous,* spawning in fresh water but living in the sea. Trout are usually exceptions to this.

At spawning time, Pacific salmon return to the same river in which they were hatched. How they manage to do so is unknown. The trait is probably not inherited; when eggs laid in one stream are transferred to another, as adults the salmon return to the stream where they hatched, and not to the one in which their parents spawned. Some experiments indicate that the salmon's keen sense of smell may be involved. Their homing ability seems to be lost if the nostrils are plugged.

The trip to the spawning place may take as long as a year. They usually do not feed on this trip. When they arrive, females make nests called *redds,* depressions about a foot (.3 meter) deep in the riverbed. Fertile eggs develop there. A female may make several redds in a series going upstream.

After five to six months, eggs hatch into *elevins* that live on stored yolk for several weeks. Young salmon, called *parr,* live and feed in the river from one to five years. When they are ready to return to the sea, they are known as *smolt.* After one to five years of marine life, they return to the river as mature adults to spawn.   J. C. K.

SEE ALSO: SPAWNING

Salsify see Oyster plant

WILL SALT CONDUCT ELECTRICITY?

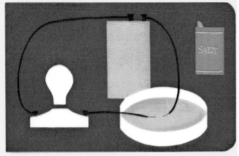

1 Connect a small bulb to a dry cell with bell wire. Fasten a second piece of wire to the remaining terminal of the bulb receptacle and lead the exposed end of it to the dish of water. Connect a third wire to the other terminal of the dry cell and lead it to the dish. The two wires in the water may be an inch or two apart.

2 Does the bulb light up? Mix a tablespoon of table salt into the water. What happens now? Dissolve a second tablespoon of salt in the solution. Does the bulb burn brighter?

3 Salt contains negatively charged chloride and positively charged sodium ions. A stream of electrons flow from the chloride to the sodium ions. Experiment with other materials such as sugar, baking soda, and vinegar. Are they electrolytes?

SOME SALTS USED IN EVERYDAY LIFE

Chemical and Common Name	Molecular Formula	Principal Uses
Potassium aluminum sulfate (Potash alum)	$K_2Al_2(SO_4)_4$	Hardens pickles; skin astringent
Aluminum sulfate	$Al_2(SO_4)_3$	To acidify too-alkaline soils, in fertilizers
Calcium hypochlorite (Chloride of lime)	$CaCl_2O$	In weak solution, to bleach cloth (corrosive to hands)
Sodium chloride (Table salt)	$NaCl$	Needed in human foods to preserve or "pickle" foods
Potassium hydrogen tartrate (Cream of tartar)	$KHC_4H_4O_6$	In candy and desserts, to prevent sugar crystals
Sodium nitrite (Nitrite of soda)	$NaNO_2$	Both salts used to preserve red hemoglobin in meats
Sodium Nitrate (Nitrate of soda or Bengal salt peter)	$NaNO_3$	
Sodium benzoate (Benzoate of soda)	$NaOOC.C_6H_5$	To retard bacterial growth in starch pastes, and foods
Sodium bicarbonate (Baking soda)	$NaHCO_3$	As leavener with sour milk in baking; as stomach alkalizer; to make baking powder (with a dry acid-salt)
Magnesium sulfate (Epsom salts)	$MgSO_4$	Strong, mineral laxative; in solution, to soak muscle-sore limbs

Salt Salt usually refers to the seasoning used for flavoring or preserving food. It is, however, just one of a large group of substances which, in chemistry, are called salts. Most other salts are poisonous and are not used for food purposes but are used in industry and agriculture.

Salts are combinations of two ions, one a metallic ion. By substitution of hydrogen in an acid, a salt is formed. Commonly, the reaction of an acid plus a base yields a salt and water. The acid always contains a hydrogen ION (H^+) and the base, an hydroxyl ion (OH^-), the two of which together produce water. This process is called *neutralization,* as both acidic and basic characteristics are eliminated. Thus, hydrochloric acid reacts with sodium hydroxide forming water and table salt, sodium chloride, as follows:

$$HCl + NaOH \rightarrow H_2O \text{ (water)} + NaCl \text{ (salt)}.$$

Under some circumstances, salts may contain a hydrogen ion in addition to the other positive ion. This is an acid salt as in sodium hydrogen sulfide, $NaHSO_4$. If a hydroxyl ion is present in addition to the usual negative ion, a basic salt exists as in baking soda, $NaHCO_3$. Most salts have crystalline structures.   D. J. I.

SEE ALSO: CHEMISTRY

Saltpeter Common saltpeter is *potash niter,* mined where ancient living remains were buried by sediment. It is purified and used mostly in making fireworks, black gunpowder, matches and as fertilizer.

Potash niter (or potassium nitrate) also has uses in preserving color in meats. It is mined on all continents. The other niter is *sodium nitrate,* commonly called *Chile saltpeter* after the abundant deposits found in coastal Chile.

Both kinds of saltpeter, when pure, are formed in water-clear rhombic or trigonal crystals. The salts are highly soluble in water. In taste they resemble unpleasantly flavored table salt. Sodium nitrate has the formula $NaNO_3$; the formula of potassium nitrate is KNO_3.   D. A. B.

Saltwater see Brine, Oceanography, Sea water

Salve A salve is a thick, sticky ointment which is applied to wounds and sores. It is used as a soothing and healing agent, or to hold medicine which must be applied locally.

Helen J. Challand
Salvia

Salvia (SAL-vee-uh) A whole group of HERBS is called salvia. Another name for these highly scented flowering plants is sage.

LEAVES are simple and opposite. The square stem is 1-8 feet (.3-2.4 meters) high. Perfect FLOWERS have five petals and sepals, four stamens, and one pistil. Their colors are blue, red, yellow, or white. FRUIT is made of four one-seeded nutlets. Salvia is in the Lamiaceae family.   H.J.C.

Samarium (suh-MAIR-ee-um) Samarium is the 62nd element, and is part of a group known as the *rare earth elements*. Samarium belongs to the lanthanide, or cerium, series of elements, and is the hardest metal of the lanthanide group. It is yellow in color.

Salts of samarium, such as the oxide, hydroxide, chloride, and sulfate are known. The metal itself is usually purified from one of its salts by reduction. It will oxidize when left exposed to the oxygen of the air.

Samarium (symbol Sm) has atomic weight 150.35.   M. S.

SEE ALSO: ATOM, ELEMENTS

Sand Sand is a common earth material that is found in all parts of the world. It is formed as rocks are broken down by erosion and weathering. Most sand is made of the mineral QUARTZ.

Most sand results from the decomposition of GRANITE, and contains the minerals

Photo courtesy Society for Visual Aids, Inc.

Sand is bits of eroded rock.

FELDSPAR and quartz. Often it contains dark colored minerals like MAGNETITE and hornblendes. Dark sand like that of the famous black sand beaches of Hawaii are composed of OLIVINE. Sand is an important material used in the making of glass, abrasives, cement, and certain types of plaster. Precious metals such as gold and diamonds are often associated with sand deposits.   P.P.S.

SEE ALSO: ABRASIVE, CEMENT, EROSION GLASS, OCEAN, ROCKS

Sand dollar These are spiny-skinned animals that look either like a wheel with spokes or like a star. They are flattened from top to bottom (*dorsoventrally*) like a cookie, and are sometimes called sea cookies. Sand dollars move and bury themselves in the sand by digging with their spines. Their *tube feet* are used in locomotion.

Tube feet work in relays by changes in water pressure. Movement is very slow. The mouth is in the center of the ventral side and is surrounded by pyramid-shaped teeth. They feed on the debris in the sand which drops between the spines on the dorsal surface. Food is carried by cilia to the margins or edges of the body. It enters the ciliated grooves containing the tube feet (*ambulacral grooves*) and is swept into the mouth. The intestine follows the circumference of the shell (*test*) and ends in an anus on the edge. Both sexes look alike.   J. C. K.

SEE ALSO: ECHINODERMATA, SEA URCHIN

Sand dune see Dune

Sand verbena see Wild flowers

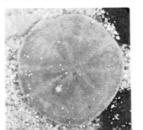

Sand dollar on sea bottom

Courtesy Society For Visual Education, Inc.

Sandalwood

Sandalwood There are two kinds of sandalwood. Red sandalwood is an East Indian tree. Its wood is hard and fragrant. The other kind of sandalwood grows wild in India. Oil distilled from it is used in perfumes and medicines.

A natural red plant dye is extracted from the sap of the red sandalwood tree. The other sandalwood is cultivated in parts of Europe and Asia. The sweet scent of this tree comes from oils and resins in the HEART-WOOD. This odor repels insects, making the lumber valuable for chests and boxes. This species of sandalwood belongs to the family Sandalaceae, while red sandalwood is in the family Leguminosae. H. J. C.

Sandarac (SAN-duh-rak) Sandarac is the pale-yellow transparent resin of the North African sandarac tree. The sweet-smelling resin is used in varnish and as incense. The sandarac tree is a member of the PINE family, and has a hard wood used in building.

Sandbars are a danger to ships because they are difficult to see

Sandbar A sandbar is a ridge of sand, usually submerged under water. Sandbars are found in rivers, lakes, and oceans. They are formed when fast moving water which carries sand suddenly slows down. Sandbars are very dangerous to ships. Many ships are wrecked or run aground on sandbars.

Almost all rivers contain sandbars. In floods and in the parts of rivers with swift currents, sand is picked up by the fast moving water. When the water slows further downstream, it no longer is able to carry the sand. Thus the sand settles to the bottom and gradually piles up to form a growing sandbar.

Larger rivers, such as the Mississippi, have many sandbars which are a hazard to river boats. The sandbars are marked with navigational buoys to warn the boats from running aground. Because of floods on a river, sandbars change their position, creating new hazards for boats.

Waves and winds stir sand on the bottom of lakes and oceans. These forces cause the water to carry the sand to the calmer water nearer shore. Sandbars are formed. If enough sand is piled up, an island or a chain of sand islands may develop. The water remaining between the mainland and the sandbar island is a *lagoon*. P. F. D.

Sandblast Sandblast is a stream of sand or other small particles driven by compressed air or steam. It is used to clean such hard surfaces as metal or stone, or to etch glass. Frosted glass is made by sandblasting glass covered with a stencil of the desired design.

Sandpaper see Abrasive

Sandpiper

Sandpiper Sandpipers are wading birds of medium size. They belong in a family that includes woodcocks, snipes, and godwits. Most of them are rather drab with brown or grayish feathers on their backs and white on their bellies. There are around 45 species in North America.

Sandpipers wade into water to catch living prey but are also important beach *scavengers*. They clean beaches of many small animals that have washed ashore. Often they are pests near open breeding pools at hatcheries.

Nests are laid upon the ground, and are shallow depressions scantily lined with grass. Three or four eggs are laid. Young hatch from the eggs at the same time and do not remain in the nest as *nestlings*.

After the breeding season is over, sandpiper pairs are no longer solitary but rather congregate in large flocks.   J. C. K.

SEE ALSO: SNIPE

Sandstone see Rocks

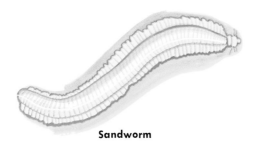

Sandworm

Sandworm Sandworms are *segmented* (in rings) WORMS burrow on the sandy sea bottom. They may be 15 inches (38 centimeters) long. Along their sides are fleshy lobes or *parapodia* used for movement and breathing.

Sandworms have a closed circulatory system (the blood is always inside of a vessel). The mouth opens into a jawed *pharynx*. This can be pushed out of the mouth to tear off pieces of algae with the teeth. Behind the pharynx is an *esophagus, stomach-intestine,* and *anus*. For excretion of waste, sandworms have a type of kidney called a *nephridium*. The nervous system is like that of typical ANNELIDA. There are several sense organs such as tentacles for touch, eyes for sight, and palps around the mouth for taste.

Sexes are separate, but sex organs are not permanent. Sex cells are budded off and shed through nephridia (the body wall). Eggs develop into TROCHOPHORE larvae.   J. C. K.

Sanitation Sanitation is the study and use of methods that help to protect health and prevent disease.

Since the natural openings in the body, such as the mouth and nose, are potential places for the entry of bacteria, much of sanitation is connected with prevention of bacteria which enter the body and affect health. Inspection of food, PASTEURIZATION of milk, filtration of water, disposal of sewage, chemical control of disease-carrying insects, and vaccination against communicable diseases are a few of the safety measures that are involved in sanitation.

Although the U. S. Public Health Service is the national organization concerned, smaller state and local health organizations also study sanitation, enforce rules and educate the public.   E. P. L.

SEE ALSO: PASTEUR, LOUIS; PUBLIC HEALTH; SEWAGE DISPOSAL; TYPHOID FEVER

Sansevieria (sann-sih-VEER-ee-uh) Sansevieria is a common house plant. Its long green leaves grow directly from an underground stem. The plant has no stem above ground. It grows easily with little care or sun.

The fragrant flowers are whitish to yellow. They bloom in an open cluster on a tall flower stalk. The fruit is a berry with 1 to 3 seeds. Leaves grow as long as 8 feet (2.4 meters) and as wide as 3 inches (7.6 centimeters). The plant is propagated by division of RHIZOME and by leaf cuttings. The variegated types may produce only plain green leaves when propagated by cuttings.

Sansevieria was named after a Prince of Sanseviero who was born in Naples, Italy, in 1710. It is sometimes called *snake plant*.

Sansevieria belongs to the lily family. It has fifty species in Africa and Asia. P. G. B.

Sapodilla see Chicle

Sansevieria

Saponification Saponification means the changing of an animal or vegetable fat by reaction with an alkali. *Soap* (a mixture of fatty acids) and glycerol are the products of the reaction.

J. Daniel Willems

Synthetic star sapphire

Sapphire Sapphire is a precious stone. Like a diamond, it is very valuable. Most sapphires are a transparent blue, though some come in other colors.

Sapphires are found in many parts of the world. The cornflower blue stones of Kashmir, northern India, are the most precious and beautiful. Those of Ceylon are paler in color and not so valuable. Sapphires found in Australia are a dark blue in the daylight but become almost black in artificial light. Other sources include Thailand, Burma, and Montana in the United States.

Sapphires are classified as CORUNDUMS. Those of other colors, such as red, are known as rubies.   D. E. Z.

SEE ALSO: GEM, RUBY

Saprophyte (SAP-ro-fite) Plants may be grouped according to their food habits. Saprophytes are plants that live off of dead things.

Saprophytes are animals that eat dead organisms. Saprophytic FUNGI absorb food in solution through a system of filaments. BACTERIA take it in by osmosis through their cell walls.   H. J. C.

Sapsucker Sapsuckers are a group of American WOODPECKERS. They have the unusual habit of making long rows of holes in the bark of trees. They drink the sap that oozes out of the holes and eat the insects that have been attracted to it. They eat great numbers of insects and also fruit. Sometimes the bark of the tree is de-

Sapsucker

stroyed when they make holes in it, and the tree dies. This is often the case with fruit trees.

Sapsuckers live mainly in forests with small clearings and near water. They build their nests in a dead or dying tree that is close to water. They scoop out a cavity about a foot (.3 meter) deep, leaving an opening just large enough for them to enter. They lay five or six white eggs.

They are about 9 inches (22.9 centimeters) long, attractively colored in black, white, red, and yellow. The yellow-bellied sapsucker is beautifully colored and easily recognized by most bird watchers.   M.R.L.

Sapwood Sapwood is the younger and softer wood just inside the bark of trees. It often surrounds a center core of dark HEARTWOOD. New sapwood is added each year. It is the youngest of the xylem tissue.

Sapwood is most active in conducting raw materials and storing food. It is usually lighter than heartwood, less durable, and not as valuable for lumber. It is also more susceptible to attack by insects.   H. J. C.

SEE ALSO: HEARTWOOD

Saran see Plastics

Sarcoma see Cancer (disease)

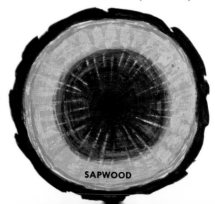

SAPWOOD

Sardine

Sardine This is the commercial name for any small fish packed in oil. They are often called *pilchards* and belong in the HERRING family. They are silver with a narrow body width. Sardines are PLANKTON feeders, traveling in schools in the open sea.

Pilchards have oily flesh. The dorsal fin is centrally placed. The second rayless, more posterior dorsal fin is missing. This fin is called the *adipose fin.* The fork in the tail fin is deep. Scales of the body form a sharp ridge along the center of the ventral side. Scales are *deciduous,* falling off at the slightest touch. Because of this, pilchards do not live long in an aquarium.

Their mouths are almost toothless. Planktonic organisms get caught on the *gill rakers* in the throat. The mouth acts like a siphon.

Most pilchards spawn in shallow water in the spring or summer. Eggs are laid on seaweed and other surfaces. These fish have long lives, some living up to eleven years. J. C. K.
SEE ALSO: HERRING

Sargassum (sahr-GASS-um) Sargassum, a curious form of seaweed, has given its name to a large area of the Atlantic Ocean. The *Sargasso Sea,* which legend has made famous, is not really a sea, but part of the ocean which lies under a perpetual calm.

Bounded on the north by a line from Chesapeake Bay to Gibraltar, and on the south by a similar line from Haiti to Dakar, it reaches from Bermuda to more than half-way across the Atlantic. No one knows positively how the brown algae came to grow so thickly in this warm, very salty, sluggish part of the ocean. Some marine biologists believe that many of the plants are torn loose from their rocky shelters by the Gulf Stream. As the plants float northward and eastward, finally drifting into the Sargasso, they carry with them a host of "passengers"—small fish, crabs, shrimp

Sargassum

and other forms of marine animals. Over the centuries these animals have adapted themselves to the floating homes provided by the sargassum weeds.

It is thought that once the sargassum reaches the area, it may live for centuries. Although some of the plants die on the fringes of the Sargasso because of unfavorable conditions, new plants do appear each year. It has been estimated that perhaps 10 million tons (9 million metric tons) of the algae float lazily over the area.

During the days of the early explorers, it was believed that the weed was so thick that it could seize and hold a ship until the ship rotted away under the blazing sun. This is only superstition, for the weed grows in clusters and is nowhere thick enough to stop the passage of even a very small vessel. Many fanciful tales grew up around this superstition, but none were true.   R. N. J.
SEE ALSO: CURRENTS, OCEAN; GULF STREAM; PELAGIC; SEA WATER

Sassafras (SASS-uh-frass) The funny-sounding name, sassafras, is that of a tree which grows in the eastern United States. An oil extracted from sassafras, *safrole,* is used in flavoring and perfumes.

The unique sassafras tree has three different kinds of leaves on one twig. They are the mitten-shaped leaf, the oval, and the three-lobed leaf. A delicate fragrance comes from the tree and the dark-green twigs have a pleasant, spicy taste. The fruit is a deep-blue drupe. In the autumn, the leaves turn brilliant flame or yellow. J. K. K.

Sassafras leaves

Conversion Factors to Metric Measurement

Length

1 inch = 25.4 millimeters (mm) exactly
1 inch = 2.54 centimeters (cm) exactly
1 foot = 0.3048 meters (m) exactly
1 yard = 0.9144 meters (m) exactly
1 mile = 1.609344 kilometers (km) exactly

Area

1 square inch = 6.4516 square centimeters (cm^2) exactly
1 square foot = 0.092903 square meters (m^2)
1 square yard = 0.836127 square meters (m^2)
1 square acre = 0.404686 hectares (ha)
1 square mile = 2.58999 square kilometers (km^2)

Cubic Measure

1 cubic inch = 16.387064 cubic centimeters (cm^3) exactly
1 cubic foot = 0.0283168 cubic meters (m^3)
1 cubic yard = 0.764555 cubic meters (m^3)

US Liquid Measure

1 fluid ounce = 29.5735 milliliters (ml)
1 fluid ounce = 0.2957 deciliters (dl)
1 pint = 0.473176 liters (l)
1 gallon = 3.78541 liters (l)

US Dry Measure

1 pint = 0.550610 liters (l)
1 bushel = 35.2391 liters (l)

Weight

1 grain = 0.0647989 grams (g)
1 ounce = 28.3495 grams (g)
1 pound = 0.453592 kilograms (kg)
1 short ton = 0.907185 metric tons (t)
1 UK ton = 1.01605 metric tons (t)

Temperature

To convert Fahrenheit to Centigrade (Celsius) complete the following
equation. $(F° - 32) \times 5 \div 9 = C°$